JILLIAN TEDESCO

Founder and CEO of fit-flavors

OWNING *the* WAIT

Harnessing Your Spirituality and Mindset

OWNING THE WAIT © copyright 2022 by Jillian Tedesco. All rights reserved. No part of this book may be reproduced in any form whatsoever, by photography or xerography or by any other means, by broadcast or transmission, by translation into any kind of language, nor by recording electronically or otherwise, without permission in writing from the author, except by a reviewer, who may quote brief passages in critical articles or reviews.

ISBN: 978-1-63489-504-0

Library of Congress Catalog Number has been applied for.
Printed in the United States of America
First Printing: 2022

26 25 24 23 22   5 4 3 2 1

Cover and interior design by Dan Pitts

Wise Ink Creative Publishing
807 Broadway St NE
Suite 46
Minneapolis, MN, 55413

CONTENTS

My Story 3

The Bible 15

My Encounter with God 19

Growing "flavors by Jillian" Out of My House 29

Taking Ownership of Mind, Body, and Spirit 49

My Nutrition Journey 57

My Nutrition Philosophy 63

The Mindset Shift 69

Visualization 77

Speaking New Narratives 87

Writing 93

Education 101

Making Time 107

Owning and Processing the Failures 113

Trusting the Process 117

What's Next 121

Dear Reader,

If you picked up this book, you are interested in bettering your nutrition and your well-being. Kudos on wanting to learn and grow—one of the biggest factors in becoming successful in anything you do. If you get to the end of this book, kudos a second time, as so many of us start books but don't finish them. With that in mind, I wanted this book to be short and impactful. I wanted to be as transparent with you as I can, because you deserve the truth. I wish someone would have taught me all of this before I stumbled in my nutrition and my career.

I originally set out to write a cookbook. But I believe God wanted me to tell my whole story, to connect with readers. I doubted myself so many times through this process, questioning if I should leave my story out, as if no one would care to read it. However, at the end of the day, I am living in faith, and I believe there is a bigger purpose for these words. After nine months of writing—and with God's guidance and nudging—my manuscript took a one-eighty and turned into a book on mindset that I am compelled to share.

In this book, I share my encounters with God. It took me years to feel comfortable enough to share them with anyone. He is the reason I started my company, He is the reason I pushed through the hardest times, and He is the reason I wrote this book for you. This book is not about God, but it is about the inner work that is necessary to learn and grow—to keep moving forward. So in that sense, this book embodies my spirit and my purpose.

I am here to share my mess-ups, my darkest fears, and the mental warfare that held me hostage for years. My only hope is that you gain insight and confidence by *owning the wait*—taking ownership of your struggles—during your own journey toward learning to harness your mindset.

Sincerely,
Jillian Tedesco

MY STORY

It is no surprise to me now that my failure was the catalyst to my growth and change. This story is the foundation of my life, the roots from which I grow. These struggles solidified my values and changed my perspective. Life with God is better.

When I look back, certain seasons of my life stand out—mainly the struggles, some where I was barely getting by. These seasons taught me valuable lessons and provided deep experiences, which were necessary to prepare me to write this book, launch a podcast, free myself of dieting, grow a family, and run a company. My hardest failure turned out to be the vehicle to fuel my pivot. After fear and failure, I learned about hope and faith, allowing me to find success and happiness. Everyone has a story, and here is mine.

We lived in Akron, Ohio, until my senior year, when my mom was transferred for work to Murfreesboro, Tennessee. I went from a busy city to a country-bumpkin suburb (talk about drastic change). I was used to boys with spiked hair and athletic clothes. But in Murfreesboro, boys chewed dip in class, stuck fishhooks in their hats, and wore camouflage Carhartts. For a seventeen-year-old girl, this transition was hard, although relocating at a young age gave me early experience with adversity. I didn't even know the names of either of the seniors I sat next to at graduation. And I had been big into athletics prior to the move—I was even offered a softball scholarship—but the hard transition and a senior slump during my softball season seemed to diminish my dreams of playing ball in college. Also, I'd been playing softball year-round since I was twelve, so I was ready for something new. So I made the hard decision to decline the scholarship and started looking for work.

I got a job at a small mom-and-pop gym recommended by my mom, of all people, and after my first set of walking lunges, I fell in love with fitness. By eighteen years old, I was certified as a personal trainer. I was obsessed with the idea of physical fitness, and I was on a mission to change my body composition. I started dating a body builder, quit eating carbs and drinking alcohol (at eighteen!), and started weighing everything I ate. I was all in. (This was the beginning of my walk down the wrong path with nutrition.)

I completed one year at Middle Tennessee State University, then dropped out. After getting certified as a trainer, I knew I did not need a degree to train successfully. I then went on to get two more certifications—exercise therapy and a specialization in sports nutrition—to boost my resume. The owner of the mom-and-pop gym I was working at in Tennessee had another gym in Miami, Florida. An opportunity presented itself for me and my boyfriend to work there, so we moved to Miami together on a whim. I was nineteen.

The job was in downtown Miami, where we ran the fitness center at the InterContinental Hotel on the corner of First Street and Biscayne Boulevard. I trained high-profile lawyers and bankers as well as hotel management staff. With regimented eating and no drinking, I was living the trainer lifestyle and making good dough. I was growing up fast and learning how to "adult."

Living down there was an experience. Every day, I would wake before the sun rose, then hit the street for some morning cardio. I often saw wild peacocks while walking around Coconut Grove. Then I'd head to the gym by 7:00 a.m. and work all day, until sunset. My boyfriend was controlling and didn't let me do much, so I rarely went out, and I only traveled to South Beach one time. This was not what one might envision for a nearly twenty-year-old living in Miami.

My relationship with my boyfriend was suffering (predictably, in retrospect). He would abuse me mentally and emotionally, always commenting on my body and work ethic and questioning everywhere I went, which made me very insecure. I was too scared to leave him at the time, so I stayed in that toxic relationship (for what would become three years). Plus, Miami was not in the cards for me solo, so as a last-ditch, misguided effort, we decided to move to St. Louis. We packed our stuff into our two-door car, made the trek, and stayed with a friend there for a few weeks, until we found an apartment.

The move did not solve our issues, but it did provide new distractions and opportunities. I briefly worked for Gold's Gym in St. Louis, then ended up working at a personal-training studio in Chesterfield, Missouri, and my boyfriend got a job there too. I also created and launched, at only twenty-one years old, a program to help people lose weight. I didn't realize it at the time, but I was setting the foundation for my nutrition philosophy and entrepreneurial spirit as well as gaining valuable firsthand experience helping clients work toward a healthier lifestyle.

Despite my success, the studio I was working at was not ethically run, and the culture was dying. After a few years there, I decided to open a separate personal-training studio with a colleague—whom we will call Mr. Eggs, because he ate a *lot* of them. We thought we could do it better, so we started planning our exit.

During the planning phase, I joined a few different local gyms to get exposure and see how they were run. I would visit their locations before I went to my studio to train clients, and that is when I first laid eyes on Jason (my husband). It was the highlight of my day. For three months, we stared at each other, never saying anything. It was like we could feel the energy through our eyes. I think I fell in love with him before I knew him. This joy kept my spirit alive during the end of my toxic relationship with my boyfriend and gave me the courage to finally leave him, two years after we'd moved, right before I turned twenty-two. I'd recently caught him in a lie about cheating, and that was the final push to end it.

A huge, dead weight was off my shoulders. Right after the breakup, I heard Kelly Clarkson's song "Since U Been Gone" on my car radio. I sang along at the top of my lungs—"I can breathe for the first time"!—and bawled my eyes out. I was able to go wherever, whenever I wanted. And during a night out with friends, I saw Jason. The next morning at the gym, I confronted him. "I know you want to talk to me," I said. He smiled. He was the kindest person I had ever met. We became inseparable that day, and after three weeks, we said we loved each other.

During a time when I wasn't necessarily looking for another relationship, Jason had swooped in and reminded me what a happy relationship could feel like. He was there to encourage and support me as I continued to work at the same studio as my ex. Jason didn't like that I was still working there, but I was making enough money that it made sense for me to stay until my new studio was ready. And I'd been driving the Nissan 350Z that my ex had set me up with (I didn't have much credit when I was twenty), and I'd made all the payments, yet when we broke up, he stole my keys and took the car, saying I had to pay him $1,500 if I ever wanted to see it again—another attempt to control me. Jason let me borrow his car full-time and said he would rent a loaner for himself until I figured out what I wanted to do.

After car shopping for a few weeks, I decided I wanted my "Z." Frustrated with how my ex was treating me, Jason wrote out a check for $1,500 and said, "Here, have him cash this." Having Jason step in like that was huge. Regardless of the cost, he wanted my ex to know that he couldn't treat me like that anymore. I thought he was crazy for writing that check, but I eventually realized he was willing to do whatever it took. I was a priority to him. Jason showed up for me, and he still does every day.

By twenty-two, I had lived in four states, run two clubs, started a weight-loss program, and was planning to open my first business. I thought I knew everything. You ever heard of the saying "young and dumb"? That is probably a good way to sum up my first huge career mistake: rushing into business with someone I didn't know. Mr. Eggs was the majority owner, and I simply jumped on board and signed the partnership. At the time, my financial investment was $60,000—all in with everything I had saved. Starting a business is a huge risk on its own, but this was like signing a marriage document, and the "divorce" would cost me.

I worked the ten-to-twelve-hour days (including weekends) typical for a business owner, yet I wasn't feeling fulfilled like I thought I should. I loved my clients and personal training, but I wanted more from my life. I remember thinking, *Who am I? What value do I add to this world? Could I do something different?* I clearly had a *what*, but I lacked a clear *why*. And that scared me, too, because nothing had purpose or reason. I was lost.

I studied nutrition and recipes between training sessions, and I cooked when I was at home. I was becoming a foodie as a result, and in my heart, I dreamed of attending culinary school, something I never thought would be possible while running my business. During the three years I worked at that studio, I dreamed of change but felt guilty about it. Plus, I'd just started the business. So I suppressed the dream.

After a couple of years in St. Louis, I was living with Jason, by then my boyfriend, so I was able to get by financially. (I like to say he fed me and gave me shelter.) I didn't pay myself for the first year in business, and years two and three, I only took a $500 monthly distribution—not what I had hoped for. Mr. Eggs and I never seemed to catch up with all the behind-the-scenes business responsibilities. The first few years consisted of us training, doing sales, and cleaning, all just to keep the place operating. This is typical for a new business, but it leaves little to no time for planning for the future.

About three years into the deal, Mr. Eggs and I started having our differences; he wanted to spend money improving the look of the space and the quality of our equipment and light fixtures, whereas I wanted to focus on marketing and advertising. We continued to butt heads, and on my twenty-fifth birthday, we had a massive falling-out. I remember sitting in our office, in total disagreement, crying and using raised voices. He had some very disheartening things to say to me, and I knew we couldn't work together anymore. The professionalism was gone, and the trust was lost, so I decided to walk away from the toxicity. I quit.

Not knowing where to go or what to do, I thought I had lost the world. I'd felt proud when I had a business, like I'd "made it"—*This is the life* . . . right? So my ego took a major hit when it was over. Even though I hadn't been making any money or been happy, I could always at least hide behind the facade of relative success: having a business and being further along in life than some of my peers. I'd had high hopes it would work. But in one day, it was all gone, and I had to face the world as a failure, as someone who couldn't figure business out. I was back at square one—twenty-five years old with no job, no formal education, and no cash.

At this point, I hadn't challenged my mind much, so I was naive in several ways: My mindset was undisciplined, and without good habits to support a change or failure, I went a little crazy, gained some weight, and let my spirit fall victim to anxiety and depression. Without God in my life, I didn't yet have the faith to give me hope. And I'd just started really diving into the science of nutrition and cooking more, so I still had a lot to learn.

> *Sometimes ugliness has to happen before beauty can be possible.*

When I look back, I see the mistakes I made: I rushed into the wrong business with the wrong person. I didn't take ownership of the business operations. I acted as if I worked for my partner and just went along with what he suggested, not truly being responsible or understanding anything. I had no formal education or experience in marketing or advertising. But even though I learned many lessons the hard way, that I learned them at all means my time there was not a complete waste. I also maintained an amazing work ethic and created loyal relationships with a lot of my clients, who followed me when I landed my next gig at the small family-owned gym around the corner. Silver lining, right?

After leaving my business, even with a new job to distract me, I fell into a dark place, developing false beliefs about who I was and what I wanted. I felt insecure and began questioning everything I'd done in my career. Anxiety followed me during the day and attacked me every night, and I had no faith to ground me. I would try to go to sleep, only to start gasping for air, sit up in bed, and tell Jason I felt like an elephant was sitting on my chest. My heart wasn't lying to me. Being with clients all day did not allow me to pursue my passion for food and nutrition like I wanted. I knew I had more to offer.

> *When we are young, there is intense pressure to know what we are going to do with our lives by the time we're seventeen. I didn't know, and it took me years to find my purpose in life. Life requires us to be resilient during adversity if we are going to find our way and feel fulfilled.*

Jason was traveling for work all the time, and my family lived in another state. I didn't have many deep friendships because all I'd done for the past three years was work. My "friends" were forty-to fifty-year-old clients. It was about four weeks after losing my business that I had a panic attack so bad I called 911, because I thought I was dying. As I waited for the ambulance to show up—alone, as Jason was on one of his business trips—I remember sweating and feeling cold at the same time. I took my pulse—220 beats per minute. My chest was closed up, I couldn't breathe, and I felt that damn elephant sitting on me again.

When the ambulance arrived, the paramedics loaded me into the back, all the while I cried out that I was having a heart attack. I remember the ride to the ER—lying on my back, cords everywhere, numerous beeps. And the times I was alone at the hospital felt like a scene from a movie. The nurse who cared for me was sweet. She calmed me and called me "honey." She said, "Honey, we ran your vitals, and they are perfect. You did not have a heart attack. You are going to live. What trauma happened to you recently?" How did she know? She assured me what I experienced was a panic attack.

This was my wake-up call. Sitting alone in a hospital bed, freaked out, I said, "This is not me. I'm not insecure and full of anxiety!" I felt so alone and desperate. Right then, when I had no one to call on, I cried out, "God, if you're real, show me! If you're real, help me! What do I do?" This was the first time I think I really needed God. It was the first time I reached out to Him in despair. What happened next changed my life forever.

> *"'For I know the plans I have for you,' declares the Lord, 'plans to prosper you and not harm you, plans to give you hope and a future.'"*
> — JEREMIAH 29:11

My mom is loving, patient, selfless, and encouraging to everyone she comes in contact with. Most people who meet "Momma Mary" love her. I have a clear picture of her when I was growing up. She would sit in our rocking chair early in the morning in her blue terry bathrobe and read her Bible. She would write Bible verses on flashcards to help her memorize them—in fact, she had Bible verses all throughout our home—and she wrote prayer requests in a notebook. And she made me attend church with her, even if I just slept in the sanctuary, which I did, with my UCLA hoodie pulled over my head. I now realize my mother did the best thing she could ever do for me: she showed me, not just told me, the way to peace—spending quiet time alone with God.

As I sat in the hospital bed, I pictured my mom in our rocking chair and wondered, *If I sat in a chair and prayed, would God talk to me?* I decided to put my heart and spirit into finding answers and made time to be alone. I did what she did—got quiet and started reading.

I have found the greatest clarity and peace in my time alone with God. It has been a vital part of my life to this day, and if you are missing peace or answers in your life, the answer is Him. It is always Him.

The Purpose Driven Life, by Rick Warren, was the first book I picked up. Years prior, a client had given it to me (her note is still inside). Warren wrote about the things that keep people from moving forward with their love for God, specifically listing fear, guilt, materialistic things, anger, and a need for approval—all of which I was experiencing. Initially, I thought it ironic and funny that I'd already owned the book, but the thing is, it's neither funny nor ironic; God knows when you are willing and ready to seek Him out, and He will reveal Himself to you. God knows your heart.

I decided to take a stab at the model of faith my mom so beautifully practiced.

THE BIBLE

*It is a powerful lesson to walk in faith,
and each time faith shows up,
it shows up differently.*

Familiarizing myself with the Bible was a big step. Although extremely intimidated, I began writing down inspiring verses, praying, and journaling. My journal was my therapist. I wrote my anger on those pages. I cried tears on those pages. And as I continued to look to God for guidance, I started to find hope through His word. It was as if the stories in the Bible were written to correlate to all of our lives, as if God is speaking through those words—encouraging, teaching, healing. Each story has a message that we, the reader, can take and apply to our lives.

Some days, I would spend three to four hours in this new practice. I'd taken a massive step back from my job, so I had the time. Since I was only working thirty hours a week, versus the sixty I was used to, I had loads of time to fully devote myself to finding answers on my curious mission. I loved the quiet time and the peace I was experiencing. I had a lot of resentment and anxiety to work through, and journaling about it helped me heal. The resentment was all directed toward my ex–business partner, and that fueled my anxiety and unhappiness. When you are unhappy and have hate or negativity in your life, how can you truly experience peace and love? I had to relinquish those feelings and release them.

When we allow negative thoughts or people to throw fuel on what we are trying to overcome or process, it only moves us backward. This is why choosing your influences is so important. I wanted to be influenced by love. I was going to find love and joy again in my life. I needed to if I was going to live to my full potential.

> *Resentment is a horrible feeling that eats at your spirit. When you learn to relinquish your negative feelings and encounter all the good God has for you, He offers love, peace, and joy. Some of us are just too damn stubborn to do the work or submit, so we often lose.*

I attended church for many years. I celebrated Easter and Christmas. I even took communion and knew all the books of the Bible. It felt good to believe in God; I felt like a good person. But it was much harder to welcome conviction, humble myself before the Father, and repent. Believing in God and having an ongoing relationship with Him are two totally different things. And until I fostered a personal relationship with God, I was just going through the motions. That didn't make me a bad person, but once I opted in, it was a totally different experience.

In the twelve years since I lost my business and found my faith, I have learned so much. That knowledge and experience has fueled changes in my career, spirituality, nutrition, and lifestyle. I now believe a person's *why* must come from a deep place. I found my *why*, my purpose, when I got quiet with God.

We all have it in us to find our purpose, though you may have to do some soul searching. And for some of us, like me, it requires working through unfortunate circumstances. I hope my story inspires you to make a change or overcome a fear that is lingering in your gut, and I can even give you some tools to facilitate change. I hope I awaken in you the need to feed your physical, mental, and spiritual practices in order to level up in life; to overcome failure, because it doesn't define you; to fight against adversity when it's sitting on you like a fat elephant; to walk in faith, because life with God is better; and, of course, to realize there is no set end date on your nutrition journey.

MY ENCOUNTER WITH GOD

God literally smacked me in the face using a human being. That, along with my faith, helped me pivot from a path of failure and fear to a new path of growth.

In my dire pursuit to find answers, I fully committed to looking beyond the common advice, looking to the Father Himself, the creator of the universe, the man upstairs—yes, God. At this point in my life, I believed in God and tried to be a good person. What I didn't have was an actual relationship with God or with Jesus. What's the difference, right? I hadn't thought too much about it, but every time my mom would say "born again" or "Jesus," I would cringe. It did not give me a good feeling. In fact, it kinda rubbed me the wrong way. I say this because I want you to know that it is not my goal to change you or push my ways on you. I want to share with you what I experienced.

I remember the first lesson God presented to me. I found this truth when I was reading about why Jesus died for us. Jesus forgives us for our sins regardless of what we do, and He loves us unconditionally. We can't earn this forgiveness, but it is available to anyone who opts in. That was God's gift to us when He sent His Son to Earth. We are sinners, struggling in this fallen world, but he gives us the opportunity to opt in to a relationship with Him. He forgives us for what we have done and even offers to be our refuge.

Boom—the conviction hit me! WWJD, literally? I was supposed to forgive Mr. Eggs, who had screwed me over in business, if I want to have love and peace in my life. I had to learn to let go, and Jesus was a perfect example of forgiveness. I prayed and journaled about it. *God, help me, how do I forgive someone who screwed me over, took my money, isn't going to pay me back . . . ?* Blah, blah, blah. Poor, pitiful me. I wrestled with it. If this was the way to peace, a step toward forgiveness and relinquishing anxiety, how was I to do it by myself? How was I supposed to just let go and forget? I prayed and prayed that God would change my heart. I couldn't forgive Mr. Eggs that fast without God's help. God doesn't promise that bad stuff won't happen, but what He does expect is for you to ask Him for help. He wants you to repent and humble your hardened heart to Him.

> *"Come to me, all you who are weary and burdened, and I will give you rest. Take my yoke upon you and learn from me, for I am gentle and humble in heart, and you will find rest for your souls. For my yoke is easy and my burden is light."*
> — MATTHEW 11:28–30

The next day, on my way to work, I drove past Mr. Eggs's car. Our eyes connected, and I felt an intense energy. I hadn't seen him in months, but the day after I prayed about him, I encountered him. Later that evening, he texted me. We both said how sorry we were for everything that had happened. We wished each other the best, and I remember smiling. I was so blown away by our apologies. A huge weight was lifted off me, and I could feel the joy of forgiveness. Call it what you want, but I call that an answered prayer. That was the first experience of my spiritual relationship with God, of my prayer being answered. And that allowed me to redirect my energy toward positivity and healing, away from resentment.

> *"And when you stand praying, if you hold anything against anyone, forgive them, so that your Father in heaven may forgive you your sins."*
> — MARK 11:25

I continued to read and study with renewed focus. At my new job, another gym, I worked with a man named Matt, whom I now believe was a mentor in my story. I also believe God places these people in our lives to help when we want to walk in His direction. Matt was a Christian, and he and I covered the front desk at the gym together. He was confident in his faith, something new to me, and I was intrigued. I opened up and shared my story with him, how I was working my way out of a bad place. He shared his story too. It was very dark, but it eventually led to him finding his spiritual way with God. His vulnerability was humbling and gave me added hope. He encouraged me to keep reading and seeking, specifically telling me to read the Gospels, the first four books of the New Testament.

Let me preface by saying that picking up a Bible is overwhelming. I didn't have much of an understanding of the Bible. It doesn't make sense if you have no guidance. The Old Testament is thirty-nine books of law, wisdom, history, and prophets. The New Testament is twenty-seven books about Jesus and His followers, but it refers back to the Old Testament, so it's super confusing to a new reader. Over the years, it starts to make sense—the characters, their roles, and the lessons they teach comprise stories that are beyond valuable. It has been my favorite text to study, and it is the first place I go for personal development.

The Gospels—Matthew, Mark, Luke, and John—are about the story of Jesus Christ. Starting with Matthew, I read about Baby Jesus, Bethlehem, and the three wise men who rode on camels. I was in denial. Three guys on camels ride miles across the desert to see the newborn King, in the middle of nowhere, based on prophecies, following a bright star and bringing gifts of gold, frankincense, and myrrh? *This is so farfetched!* I thought. I closed the Bible and went straight to Google. I stayed up late that night, plagued by curiosity and doubt.

I'll never forget reading, well into the early morning, about the Magi (a.k.a the "wise men")—thought to be astrologers, teachers, and/or priests—who followed a bright star to find the newborn King. The search results suggested that God may have used the wise men to draw attention to the birth of Jesus because of their stature and credibility back in those days. That's a story for another day, but the point is that I researched these three guys for hours and was questioning the Bible. I think we can agree that when we're experiencing disbelief, research is a good solution.

Matt encouraged me to continue seeking because that is what God wants us to do. When you don't have a good understanding or commitment to the word of God, it's easy to dismiss it as false or unrealistic, as you don't have the whole story—and it's a big one, for that matter. You definitely have to commit to unpacking this miraculous story to understand the message it contains. But it's easier not to, right? I was so curious, but I wasn't sure I wanted to be all holy yet, like a pastor or Bible thumper. I had to put down my notions and look for myself. Like I said, He had answered my first prayer, and I didn't doubt the relationship my mother had with Him. I just hadn't experienced it for myself.

That weekend, I went shopping at the farmers' market. After purchasing food, I walked through a section where farmers and artisans were selling their products. I stopped to purchase natural, homemade soaps. A hundred different varieties were arranged in a beautiful display, and I was overwhelmed with choices. The young girl working the table—she was maybe twelve years old—stared at me. She wore bib overalls and had dirty hair.

I said to her, "There are so many different soaps and smells—I can't pick. Do you have a favorite one?" I will never forget the way she responded, as if she herself was a messenger.

She distinctively stared into my eyes, and I felt unsteady. She was so young, yet she made such surprisingly strong eye contact. Reaching over the counter, she picked up a bar and held it in front of her face, never breaking eye contact with me. "This is my favorite soap," she stated, "frankincense and myrrh."

My mouth dropped, my eyes opened wide, and I felt my heart beating. *Maybe it's a coincidence,* I thought. Then, I looked beyond the display. The sunlight shone under the awning, directly on my face. I squinted into the warm light. The hair on my arms stood up, and I felt God Himself shining down on me, saying, "I know you are seeking me, and I know you are doubting me, too, but I am real, and I hear you, Jillian, loud and clear." It was no coincidence. And I'm sure you've already guessed—I bought the dang soap!

I went home and journaled about my experience. I couldn't quite believe that I'd had two God experiences in the same week. It was overwhelming yet exciting. I didn't know what to do or think next. *Holy cow, could the real God be speaking to me?*

> *I still have moments when I look into the sunlight and feel God looking down on me. I feel chills, and the hair on my body stands up in the presence of His spirit. Most times, I'm brought to tears by the power of our connection, and I feel thankful I am His child.*

The following week, I was working with Matt at the gym. After I filled him in on what happened, he smiled and said, "God will answer you if you seek Him."

Later that day, I was running the front counter, making smoothies and checking people in, when a woman I didn't know walked up. She looked to be about forty-five, with blond hair and a meek presence.

"Are you Jillian?" she asked timidly.

"Yes," I replied.

"You have been on my heart lately," she let out.

Not knowing the woman, I was very taken aback. She'd turned white like a ghost, but she proceeded to explain how hard it was for her to tell me this. And I was thinking, *Who are you and why are you trippin'?* It was awkward. She looked so sincere, almost as if she was giving me a message on behalf of someone else but didn't know why. She tried to maintain eye contact but kept looking down nervously. Then she slowly reached over the counter, put her hand on my forearm, and said, "God wanted me to tell you that everything is going to be okay." Then she left. I never saw her again.

Mind you, Matt saw the whole thing go down. After the

woman left, Matt smiled a big smile and approached me, laughing with joy. He stated, "You think that was hard for *you* to hear? Do you know the courage it took her to listen to God and pass that message along to you? She was obedient to God's plan."

I stood there, frozen in shock. A human being I did not know told me that God had talked to her . . . about me. I wasn't sure how I was supposed to process that. I'd never experienced anything like that in my life, nor has God since contacted me like he did with that woman. Do I selfishly wish he would? All the time! It would be a powerful and amazing experience. But that short interaction was my miracle, and it's a big part of my story.

After that experience, I started feeling relief from my fear and started to trust God more. I was able to let go of myself a bit. I let Him worry about what was next, and I focused on what I loved. It was freeing. As a result, I committed my life and my new work to Him. To this day, the choices I make and how I live my life are based on my spiritual foundation. I believe in my spirit that my business is God's business, and I'm just following His plan. I believe God cares more about my *availability* than my *ability*, otherwise He wouldn't have chosen me for this task.

> *"Cast all your anxiety on him because he cares for you."*
> — 1 Peter 5:7

I continued praying and journaling about what I was supposed to be doing with my life. I loved to cook, and I knew I was meant for more. I felt the permission and support to do what I do best—serve others (pun intended) by helping them eat better and leading with passion. I wanted so badly to help my clients overcome their most challenging hurdles: time and a lack of knowledge about healthy eating. The need was clear. So I came up with a solution.

I created a service to help my clients eat better and alleviate stress—premade, chef-inspired meals for a healthy lifestyle. I started cooking to help people, but in return, it helped *me* more. I started dreaming about what I deeply wanted, to focus more on food and less on training. *Could I go to culinary school?* I knew there would be a ton of work involved, but that excited me. This was the most pivotal point in my life. God had swooped in and said, "I got you. Trust in me, and follow your passion. Do the work, and walk in faith." So I turned the page. I continued my practice of being with Him and followed my dream.

My transition from training to cooking full-time would take three years. I knew I would have to keep my day job as a trainer, attend school at night, and launch my concept on the weekends if I wanted to do it all. At that point, it didn't bother me that I basically had three jobs—trainer, student, and weekend chef. I had so much joy wrapped up in the birth of this concept—I was on a high.

GROWING "FLAVORS BY JILLIAN" OUT OF MY HOUSE

Business challenges can feel overwhelming. Being able to lean on God is a huge blessing, and His teachings are crucial tools.

When you build something, the experiences along the way are what shape and mold you.

When I "meal prepped" my first meals, it was Labor Day weekend 2009. I had some friends over for a pool party, and they raved about my cooking. One friend asked if I would prepare meals for her for the whole week. With great excitement to showcase my culinary skill and challenge my nutritional layout, I agreed. The next week, I wrote a menu and shopped for groceries, then prepped, portioned, packaged, and delivered the meals. That is how "flavors by Jillian" (later renamed "fit-flavors") started.

Saying yes had been the first step. Within a few weeks, I was already cooking for a handful of my personal-training clients. I had many opportunities to be creative, a strong skill of mine, and work independently, another strong skill of mine. I was motivated by the freedom to do what I loved while making some cash on the side. The next step was to do the work, then eventually scale the process.

I couldn't imagine calling myself a "chef" without having run a kitchen or earned a culinary degree. To me, someone who just likes to cook is a "cook," not a "chef"—I wanted to be a capital-C Chef! Plus, having credentials would give me more credibility. Attending culinary school had been a dream of mine, and by God's grace, I was not going to let the opportunity pass by. So in January 2010, at twenty-five years old, I decided to apply at Le Cordon Bleu, a prestigious culinary school. Even though going to school at night on top of my day job would be hard work, that didn't matter, as I was excited about this new beginning. While applying for school, I also entered a cooking competition to win a grant, and I took third place. (Talk about an early boost to my self-esteem!)

On my first day, during my class on knife skills, I cut myself, and it was bad. I ended up with a fat, bandaged thumb covered with a blue latex "finger condom" (finger cot). Despite injuring myself—and what chef hasn't accidentally cut themself?—school was fun, and I learned skills that a lot of home cooks just don't have. I'll never forget making béchamel sauce from scratch, cooking duck confit, and cutting lardoons from a pigs' belly, among others. And we learned the logistics of each technique, which would later serve me greatly in running our company. Cooking techniques are hard enough to manage when you're cooking for a small group. But when you scale them, they are even harder to execute.

> *Going back to school is an investment of time and energy, but if you have a plan, it's just a step in the process.*

Mondays through Thursdays, I was training clients at the gym during the day and attending school in the evenings until 10:30 p.m. Combined with personal cheffing on the weekends, I would spend around one hundred hours working each week, which left me very tired. As a result, I found myself not exercising as much and eating much later in the day (late night) than I normally would, usually during or after class. I was also drinking an energy drink by 3:00 p.m. most days. As I kept up this schedule, losing muscle and gaining fat was inevitable. (This is a prime example of how we can start to slip when trying to achieve or level up. In order to grow, you must stretch yourself out of your comfort zone and welcome imbalance. Then, once equilibrium sets back in, you can reinstate all the good practices that fell to the wayside during the time of growth.)

On Fridays, I didn't have school, so I would train clients in the morning, then go grocery shopping. Friday nights were not spent out with friends but at SHOP 'n SAVE and

Costco, with food prep going late into the night. Saturdays, I cooked until midnight, and I made deliveries on Sundays. My three-day "weekends" easily added another forty hours of work. (It's hard missing those Friday and Saturday nights when you're young, but that was another sacrifice I knew would serve me later.)

I remember thinking, *This is only for ten months. I need to fully immerse myself in school and not guilt myself.* I managed to maintain most of my good habits. I was just tired every day—and eating blueberry pie or pasta at school at 10:00 p.m. (Blueberry pie was the one dish I totally bombed in school. My pie filling was runny, and my crust was soggy. I don't care for baking—too many rules and measurements that are nonnegotiable, not good for a creative person with ADD. Cooking is more forgiving, with tons of room for innovation and improvisation.) At the end of ten months, I was proud to graduate from the program; it gave me a sense of pride that carried over into our quality products, high standards, and culinary excellence.

I continued hitting my system hard for three years, and my business grew slowly but consistently. By the end of that time, I had nine refrigerator-freezer units in my house, five people working with me (including Jason), and 120 clients. On a typical Saturday, I would cook 650 meals—with a single oven. I know that sounds impressive, but it took me time to get there. Not all of those 120 clients would order every week, but they were on my list of contacts.

Each Tuesday, I would craft a new menu of twelve meals and three snacks. This was a good exercise for me. Week after week, I was challenged to create and manage the production of new and interesting recipes, and I got regular feedback from my clients. (Some of the most popular dishes from that time are still on the fit-flavors menu today.) However, I was not savvy with computers—probably because I never used one in high school and dropped out of college—so the administrative side of my business was pretty low-tech, especially by today's standards: I carried my client list with me all week. I would process orders sent via email and communicate with clients via text, only to organize all orders on paper anyway—basically a handwritten spreadsheet.

My weekly deadline for accepting orders was 8:00 p.m. on Thursday. On Thursday afternoons, I would often find myself with only forty to fifty orders—which put me into total freak-out mode. Knowing I could usually get about eighty orders, I did what I knew how to do: I hustled. At about 2:00 p.m. on Thursdays, I would hound sixty to seventy clients from my list, reminding them to order through text messages. I'm not joking. I like to think I was holding them accountable to eating well.

A valuable lesson I learned is that successful people are busy, and they often need help with the small things, such as ordering meals for the week. I never left the ball in their court. I was either closing orders or getting direct *no*s, which was good, because a *no* is better than nothing.

I did whatever I had to do to close orders, offering truly white-glove service and making suggestions where I thought it would make their lives easier: I had about twenty clients who shared their house keys with me, and I had about fifty garage codes stored in my phone—allowing me to deliver straight to their refrigerators. If clients were travelers, I would suggest they order ten meals and freeze half of them for the following week. I even started offering a Cryovac option (vacuum-sealed packaging) just to get more sales. I let clients' dogs out when I delivered food to their homes. I delivered to high-rises downtown, paying for parking and walking orders to the thirtieth floor, sometimes going straight to the break room, filling the fridge with meals, and leaving. Many of the doctors and lawyers I delivered to never even met me in person, although our text dialogue was open because I was their personal chef. I loved it.

> *When building a business, work ethic matters more than you can imagine. Each contact, transaction, and conversation helped me establish the values and standards for my business and provided a lot of practice to prepare me for something much larger that God had in store.*

One weekend, my mom and dad came up to visit Jason and me. Typically when family visits, you might do some sightseeing and go out to dinner. But for us, when my parents arrived that Thursday, we drove to Restaurant Depot. (Nothing like a quick stop at Depot after getting off the plane!) The next day, I was in full throttle. I saw my parents as two healthy, willing (?) humans that I could put to work. We were still spending time together, right?

We hit all three grocery stores in the morning. I made my dad push the carts, and Mom read the lists and checked off items. You know those big apple and pear boxes with the handles from the produce department at Costco? Yeah, those were great for my shopping excursions. I selected eight boxes and quickly placed them on the flatbed cart, placing the items SKU side up in the boxes. This was to strategically make checkout a flash with the SKU gun. I said my hellos to all the Costco employees, as they all knew me by name and were eager to help in my shopping. I had become friends with the guys in the meat department, because most weeks, I would purchase fifty to seventy-five pounds each of chicken, beef, and turkey. When we reached the register, an employee said, "Look out— she's here!" (Happened every time, without fail.) The cashier then handed me their SKU gun and let me scan my entire cart myself. (Again, I was a regular.) We had gotten in and out of Costco in thirty minutes and spent over $1,000, with everything neatly organized in those large boxes (#WINNING).

My parents were flabbergasted by my sense of urgency, but I ensured them that if I didn't hustle, I wouldn't have enough time to get it all done. Food prep started Friday afternoon and continued late into the night. The next morning, Mom helped with additional food prep and packaging meals—I kept referring to her as my sous chef. Dad did dishes all day and just yelled, because he's Italian. I think their minds were blown that weekend. They were such good sports, too!

When my house was overrun by fit-flavors, I pushed production to the max. On a cold January day, one could often find me wearing full snow gear and using my gas grill to grill and bake. (We only had one oven, so I had to improvise.) During the colder months, when the temp dropped below forty-two degrees Fahrenheit, I used my garage as a walk-in cooler. I was able to quickly cool chilis, soups, and mashed potatoes that were in large plastic food-storage containers. We also stirred food with these large cooling wands that are like spatulas full of frozen water. These techniques and practices made our last several months cooking out of the house manageable, as the meal orders had continued to grow significantly over the last year. Our business was clearly outgrowing our home.

During the warmer months, without the garage serving as a walk-in, I was forced to strategically move hot foods from one refrigerator or freezer to the next. These were standard units, so no one of them could adequately cool a sixty-serving container of mashed potatoes on its own, which made practicing ServSafe regulations even more challenging. But I found a way by playing "musical freezers." And when I ran out of space, I would just buy another freezer—that simple. It was easy to justify at the time, as my business was growing steadily.

I don't understand why people make excuses not to solve relatively simple problems with obvious solutions. When a business is first getting started, you just have to learn what works for you (it's all relative). And creating too much comfort for yourself early on won't breed growth or resilience, but having the tools you need for day-to-day operation isn't negotiable. If you need it, the answer is always *yes*. Later, when you have experience and data to inform your decisions, you can better determine what is a *maybe* or even a *no*.

During our last year doing business out of the house, things really picked up. I sourced induction burners to set up in my dining room, on a stainless-steel kitchen table I purchased from a closing business. We used those burners to blanch all our veggies and pastas. Before arriving at my house, the girl assigned to blanching would swing by the gas station and pick up twenty pounds of ice, which we used to shock the veggies and keep them bright in color. We blanched and then shocked hundreds of pounds of veggies every week. And I had another friend that just did dishes—all day.

The walls of what would be considered the formal living room in my house were lined with fridges and stock shelves, with a four-by-eight-foot plywood "table," held up by two yellow plastic sawhorses from Home Depot, serving as the packaging area in the middle of the space. If we needed more space, we opened folding tables. As I mentioned, packaging was my husband's job. For eight hours of his weekend, Jason would package all the food for flavors by Jillian because he believed in what I was doing. At that time, Jason still had his full-time job, yet he gladly sacrificed nearly all of his time off to help me package and deliver meals. On Sundays, it took all day to make deliveries, but he would ride with me just so we could be together. If you are in a relationship and are trying to build anything great, your partner needs to be supportive, otherwise your relationship is going to face challenges.

Jason and I tied the knot in September 2012 and visited my parents in Murfreesboro that Thanksgiving. We shared stories of the business—the meal counts and how much I loved the work. I remember sitting at my parents' kitchen table, eating a bowl of cereal, when Jason said, "Jillian needs to get this business out of our house. It's taking over!" He also stated he'd found a business similar to mine based in Houston, Texas, that produced thousands of meals a day and had retail locations.

My first response was "Hell no! I don't want another storefront. I failed at that."

He assured me that it would be different, it would be ours, and we would run it differently than the studio I'd opened with Mr. Eggs. I think he believed in me more than I believed in myself at the time. When we got home from Murfreesboro, we boarded a plane to Texas to do some research, filled with excitement.

Visiting this young company was an eye-opening experience. Aside from having a solid operation, they'd managed to scale it substantially with the help of investors. Suddenly, the world felt so much bigger. There was so much market out there, and if I could gain a small percentage of that market share, I could make this work! When that realization clicked, I said, "Heck, let's do it!" Why couldn't this concept be the next St. Louis Bread Co.?

> *If you think you want to do something, challenge yourself to do something uncomfortable that will get you closer to that goal. Once you do it, confidence starts to blossom.*

We got home and started planning out financials, location, equipment, etc., though the most important thing to find before we opened was the right partner. When I was in culinary school, I'd needed an externship in order to graduate. I chose to do mine at a country club close to our home. I loved that experience. When I was there, I worked in an à la carte kitchen that catered huge parties. They partnered me with the sous chef, Chris Tucker (or just "Tucker"), who, in my opinion, was one of the most upbeat and fast moving people I'd been around. He had a refreshing sense of professional urgency, and his kitchen knowledge was unending—I was impressed. He conducted and led the whole kitchen staff, and he was cool too. I loved his work ethic, and we totally clicked.

At school, I'd been taken aback by the lackadaisical discipline of my peers and even my teachers. I remember feeling like an outsider because I took it so seriously and was already doing my own thing, which no one seemed to care about. One of my teachers snarked at me when I told him what I was doing with my personal-chef business. He'd lost his restaurant and was bitter about it. He told me not to waste my time, that I should work for an establishment that was reputable. (Talk about a hater!) But not Tucker. He showed sincere interest in what I was building and always asked me questions. He was proud of me, too, even though he'd yet to see my operation in person. We shared a mutual respect (which remains the foundation of our partnership today).

Outside of my home kitchen, I was an inexperienced chef with no real commercial-kitchen experience. Tucker was my mentor and teacher, and he showed me the ropes of kitchen life. He'd met me when I was cooking two hundred meals on the weekends, but we stayed in touch throughout my time at Le Cordon Bleu. In March 2013, I asked him to meet me at 14842 Clayton Road. As we stared at the empty white space measuring about three thousand square feet, I told him I was building a kitchen and would sell my premade meals out of there. I told him that I couldn't imagine anyone but him running our kitchen, and that I wanted him to be our executive chef. With nothing but a mutual respect and a previous externship to base his decision on, he agreed to partner up. I believe God helped make that happen.

Today, Chef Tucker oversees fit-flavor's entire production facility, managing our kitchen (including an executive chef and multiple sous chefs), packaging, and distribution departments—everything that keeps the place running—with partial ownership of the company. He has always acted as a true partner, and I couldn't ask for a better human to build this business with. Today, I even get to work with his wife, who runs our stores. Having them both as partners is amazing. This is a testament that no matter where you are in your journey of building something, each relationship matters, and the attitude and work ethic you display is what defines you and how you will be remembered. But I'm getting ahead of myself . . .

In March 2013, we wrote the business plan, moved to a rental kitchen, signed the partnership—and Jason and I got pregnant. *Shit.* Yes, *shit* is right. Not good timing. I was slinging skillets and planning the opening of a store, and now I was preggers. When we decided to commit to the business plan, we'd opted to scale our operation as much as possible before opening the brick-and-mortar. We moved everything from the house to the "Green Monster"—a big green shed, certified by the Department of Health, in the middle of a cornfield in Podunk, Missouri.

All my clients lived an hour away, so this added more challenges with time management. But the new space was way better equipped than my home, with a three-compartment sink, professional equipment, and a walk-in cooler. Our client base had continued growing, and by the time we moved into the Green Monster, I'd gotten our weekly meal count up to about one thousand meals. On any given weekend, I had eight or nine people working with me. I had a list of regular helpers, and I wasn't shy about calling my friends in to help, either. It was a mini operation that lasted just short of a year.

> *Thinking back on all the stories of flavors by Jillian, working out of the Green Monster was by far one of the most memorable. The most physically taxing and time intensive, this season of my life supercharged our operation. Enjoying the journey is something you can't take for granted.*

Man, did the Monster have its own set of challenges. As meal counts grew week over week, we had to deal with a lack of air conditioning (especially difficult in the summer months) and kitchen equipment breaking down. The garbage disposal would break one week, and the freezer the next week. And our toilet was broken almost every weekend, so we would have to go to the bathroom outside in the field. When it rained, the long dirt road that led through the field would flood, and we had to drive through a mini lake. When it snowed, our cars got stuck because no one plowed.

One night, one of the coolers went out, and we ended up losing seven hundred meals due to temperature. That was a fun convo with clients, explaining no food for the week. I fully refunded them. And the next week, I gave them all order credits, trying to wow them with customer service. Running the operation and not making money for two weeks was the biggest upset I had faced yet. On top of that, each Saturday night, out of pure fear, Jason willingly set his alarm for 2:00 a.m. He would drive out to the Monster to ensure our cooler had not gone out again. Yeah, I know—insane! We were a few months away from the first fit-flavors opening, and we couldn't risk another huge loss. The thirty-minute drive to the Monster in the middle of the night was worth a little lost sleep.

I was about seven months pregnant by the time we were going full throttle at the Monster. Tucker resigned from the country club and finally joined us, and I quickly brought him up to speed on the fundamentals of balanced cooking. I taught him portion controls and how we cooked with stocks and oils instead of butter and cream. He taught me kitchen flow and brought food vendors into the conversation, and we started thinking about sourcing. When we weren't at the Monster, we worked on the plan for our future location.

Tucker was a big help when it came to sourcing anything for the kitchen, as he had connections in the industry. I remember he had our Sysco rep meet us at my house one day to talk about starting an order. We barely met the order minimum the first time. The rep knew Tucker, so she had faith in our small business. (Today we are one of Sysco's best accounts in St. Louis, which makes me smile!)

While Tucker brought industry and production knowledge, my focus was on the products, the menu design, and the customers. At this point, Tucker and I were still doing everything manually, which was not ideal, but when you're in the thick of production—go, go, go!—it's hard to find time to streamline processes, something that helps any business flourish. If you aren't constantly getting better and working smarter, your business could plateau or even fail.

The fact that I managed all my logistics manually back then is mind- boggling today. From email correspondence with over eighty clients, to all the text messages I sent on Thursdays, to calculating portions, shopping for groceries, and determining delivery routes all over St. Louis, I was hyperfocused and bursting at the seams. (Also, my baby bump was literally popping out of my spandex.) I was definitely on a high, managing all this stuff and trying to keep it organized the best I could. (Jason and I still laugh about how, before I was set up to process credit card transactions, I would drive around with thousands of dollars in cash in my car from deliveries I made on Sundays and Mondays.)

Imagine making dinner for twenty people. How much food do you need, not yielding too much or too little? If that feels overwhelming, imagine doing it for twelve meals of seventy to one hundred servings each. At 6:00 a.m. on Fridays, I would sit down with a big cup of coffee, bust out my calculator, and start analyzing our orders. I would figure out, down to the teaspoon, how much of each ingredient I needed for the week's orders. Organizing my grocery list took four hours. But as you know, I was superefficient once I got to each store.

Every Friday, I shopped at Costco, Whole Foods, Restaurant Depot, and SHOP 'n SAVE. Toward the end of our time at the Monster, it was a race against time. I had to purchase thousands of dollars' worth of products at four different stores, drive out to Podunk, and unload two cars' worth of groceries—while preggers. And it always took two cars because we needed the extra space. Then I would have to open every package so we could prep food for the Saturday cook. I marinaded proteins, cut veggies, and made all my sauces and spice blends from scratch (and we still do today). On Fridays, we would work late into the night, only to wake up at 6:00 a.m. on Saturdays and rush back out to the Monster to cook it all. If I'd forgotten anything or needed more of certain ingredients, I'd stop at Sam's Club on the way to the Monster, because Sam's allows business members to enter at 7:00 a.m. on Saturdays, before other members. Gotta work the system!

Saturdays at the Green Monster were so much fun. It was chaos, like a busy restaurant during the dinner rush, except it was like that all day. Jason would join in the clutch around 11:00 a.m. to measure and package all the meals. By that time, he had another person helping him. One of them would write client names on the thousand or so fit-flavors stickers we used to seal meals before organizing them in our fridges.

On Sundays, we bagged everyone's orders and headed out on delivery routes. We were still offering the white-glove service of entering people's homes through garages and placing orders in refrigerators. The craziest thing was that I didn't even know most of my clients. I never even met them. They were all referrals. We were just so awesome at what we did that they kept using us. (I actually only met a lot of our longtime customers once I opened the first brick-and-mortar store years later. It was so cool to put names to faces. A ton of them still order from us today, and some still call the meals "Jillian meals." Speaking of . . .)

September 2013, we moved out of the Green Monster and opened our first brick-and-mortar location. We started producing food six days a week and were able to accept vendor deliveries; I felt like I was finally able to breathe. The workload was spread out, and my bandwidth grew tenfold.

In November 2013, Vincent Michael Tedesco was brought into this world, and a few weeks later, I was back to work, breastfeeding in the office throughout the day. I'd package food, then breastfeed. I'd label containers, then breastfeed. I'd check customers out, then breastfeed. My mom decided to retire early and relocate to St. Louis so she could help us out. She would ride to work with me and help me in the office, where Vincent would play on the floor for hours. My mom managed printing all the meal labels and helped stick them on the containers. I don't regret returning to work after only a few weeks. I was fortunate enough to have my mom there, and that was an important piece of the puzzle. She gave me the opportunity to be both a mom and a business owner.

> *Maybe you don't feel like the right person for the job that God called you to, but if He called you to it, He will equip you for it. God cares more about your **availability** than your **ability**. Are you open to what He called you to do? Will you take action?*

I remember having long conversations with God about growing my business and becoming a mom in the midst of it, scared to start both ventures at the same time but relying on my faith. There were many times during my journey I struggled as a mom and a business leader, where I let my family down and let my team down. That's a part of life—nobody's perfect. You just have to keep pressing forward. Move on and learn from each lesson and opportunity. As life goes on, you continue to grow, especially if you keep a growth mindset. I will continue to push myself out of my comfort zone, welcoming new challenges and embracing change.

———

I have been on multiple podcasts, where I shared bits and pieces of my journey—early beginnings, my encounter with God, my relationship with food, and struggles running a company:

- "Size Matters, with Andy Frisella - MFCEO27" – *Real AF with Andy Frisella* – November 2015
- "FIS30-Teach Your Children Well with Jillian Tedesco, Creator of Fit Flavors" – *Food in Session* – June 2017
- "L10Mastery - Episode #011: Jillian Tedesco - Fit Flavors CEO" – *Level 10 Mastery* – November 2017
- "E7: 'All Day Every Day' - Jillian Tedesco, Fit Flavors" – *The First 5 Podcast* – September 2018
- "Live with Purpose - Jillian Tedesco" – *YouveGotThis.jess.dj* – May 2019

- "Jillian Tedesco: Faith, Growth and Fit Flavors - OP139" – *Outside Perspective* – December 2019
- "JUST START DOING IT with Jillian Tedesco (Ep. 21)" – *Balanced and Free* – March 2020
- "97-Making money selling healthy prepared meals in your gym? - Jillian Tedesco" – *Masters in Fitness Business Podcast* – October 2020
- "Interview with Jillian Tedesco" – *Wellness Unfiltered* – November 2020
- "3 Simple Nutrition Tips with Jillian Tedesco" – *Fit Girl Talk Radio* – February 2021
- "Jillian Tedesco on Tough Love, Building Fit Flavors, Lessons from the Kitchen & 'Meats & Pots' " – *Curious Me Podcast* – February 2021
- "How to Let a Failed Business Lead to a Successful One with Jillian Tedesco" – *The Leadership Locker* – April 2021

TAKING OWNERSHIP OF MIND, BODY, AND SPIRIT

I used to think "mind, body, and spirit" sounded soft, that it was for people who didn't want to train hard or manage their diet. I was uneducated, and I felt defensive, because my friends weren't living that way.

During my years as a trainer, a chef, then a business owner, I, too, struggled with my nutrition, one of many challenges we all face. If we don't take ownership of our well-being, no one else will. You could be successful in one area, but poor health can easily lead to failure in other areas. Figuring it all out is the process that many are not willing to do the work for. Whether you are trying to make a career, go to school, or build a family, when you embrace the full spectrum of mind, body, and spirit, your route to success will be easier and more fulfilling. It is a lot of work, it doesn't happen overnight, and it's constant. But it defines who you are and who you are becoming. Your actions are just pieces of the puzzle. Let me explain.

Much like how I reframed the failure of my first business, I had to shift my mindset—from fear to faith—when it came to the food I ate. When I was younger, I was easily influenced, and I started down the wrong path with my nutrition. Unfortunately, this happens to a lot of people. We just don't know any better, and we want to trust the people who seem to know what they're doing. Reality is, we all have different needs and goals, and we need to take ownership of our health. If you don't commit, you likely won't reach your full potential. But that isn't the message that is preached to us.

The media bombards us with noise, urging us to pay for program XYZ because it's on sale and promises an easy journey, a hot body, and a rainbow at the end. *Bullshit!* It's typical for us to trust our trainer or our friend at the gym. I, too, did that when I started down this path. It feels right, and whether due to naivete or a lack of education or experience, we can default to the thought patterns of someone who claims to know what they are talking about. I'm not saying trainers don't know what they are talking about or that health coaches are not qualified, just that we shouldn't rely solely on them when making health decisions. Know *why* you are doing what you are doing.

When we put our health in someone else's hands, we are opting out of the ownership part. Ever heard "You need to be your own best advocate"? Well, this is where that statement applies. If you do not get in tune with the mental, spiritual, and physical needs of your body, you are not taking ownership, and will miss out on living up to your wellness potential. Your mind, body, and spirit are all connected. And when you realize that, you can begin to honor yourself in a way that brings health and happiness.

Let me break down what is happening when we make decisions based on a deadline, for example: when we use a deadline to motivate us to change, that date is immediately imprinted in our minds as something that will help us reach our goals. What we're really doing is training ourselves to be held accountable only for a short period of time, most likely setting unrealistic goals to help us meet that deadline. And our lifestyle probably doesn't support the results we want, so we need to set hard rules and guidelines to make ourselves feel accomplished and accountable. It's a vicious cycle.

Taking time to do the real work involves a lifestyle change. Yes, change requires sacrifice, something most of us don't want to do. I'm not talking about giving up sugar or alcohol. I'm talking about your time. Making a change involves time. And we all know that we don't have enough time as it is. "I'm busy" is my most hated line I hear from people. Yes, we are all busy, but you must make time for the change you want to make. Achieving your full potential is either a priority or it's not.

WARNING: This book is not fluff. If anything, I want to call out the bullshit you feed yourself. My life's work has been to help people get from a bad spot with health and nutrition to one that is freeing and provides confidence and results. If that is not what you want, don't bother reading any further. It's only going to get more real and raw as we go. It's the layer of shit you can't see—not the donut you ate—that stands between you and your aspirations.

We are not serving ourselves when we set a short-term deadline. We must own the process indefinitely. I have worked in the realm of health, fitness, and nutrition for nineteen years, and for the most part, everyone I know that sets short-term goals is yo-yoing with their weight. They are always talking about food or exercise or what they can't have. Here's a look-in-the-mirror question to ask yourself: do you feel that setting a deadline or a timeline for weight loss will serve you and really help you shift your well-being? In my experience, questions like that are a mind-fuck. And I've seen the consequences in my clients, friends, customers, and myself.

Owning your health is an ongoing pursuit, and it will continue to change and shift. Just as we are faced with seasons of challenges or opportunities to level up, our health is always challenged, but that doesn't mean we throw in the towel—*ever*. It's very common to have the mindset that you're either "on" or "off." With that mindset, we feel pressure to be perfect when we are "on," and when we are "off," things don't matter, and we are free to eat as we please. Personally, I hate that mentality. If you are wondering why, it's because it's polarizing. You're either feeling the pressure or you're totally relaxed. Both are wrong.

Your well-being should be something you always take into consideration—a priority—not tied to a short-term "on" mode, with sporadic "off" periods. Getting there takes time. But as you add more to your plate, little by little, only taking on what you can do consistently, you are creating a sustainable lifestyle that gets easier. This new mentality frees you of the on/off trap.

Note: So many times over the years, I've heard from customers that they are ready to "do fit-flavors." Do you see the trap they've fallen into with their approach to eating and nutrition? You don't *do* fit-flavors; it's not a diet. It's just food—you're just eating. That trap mindset is what stands between you and what you want, and I will do my best to expose that.

I feel the need to address those who may need to lose quite a bit of weight. I understand the impulse to go all in once you make up your mind about changing your life and losing weight. You join a gym and start to learn what you need to change. You start meal prepping or taking supplements. You start saying no to the things you once did regularly, because you're determined to stick to this new lifestyle. Kudos! Then comes what I've seen happen over and over: your routine changes so drastically, and everything feels so different, that your mind, body, and spirit don't have enough time to catch up. That's where you fall off—maybe missing a workout to enjoy drinks with a friend—then the guilt sinks in, which makes you want to work even harder, because you let yourself down. Maybe you schedule an extra workout and promise not to skip one again, identifying your misstep as bad or wrong. This cycle of bad and good and all or nothing just plays on repeat. Sound familiar?

Here is what I would say to someone who wants (or needs) to lose weight:

1. Understand it doesn't happen overnight.
2. It won't come off fast, at least not if you do it the healthy way—and isn't that what you really want?
3. It will require a mental commitment of one to two years minimum before it feels natural.
4. You should work with a professional. But that doesn't mean you can check out.
5. Take full ownership of your schedule, the education involved, and the time commitment.
6. Make time to work on your mind and spirit, or your body will give out.

Food is just a piece of the puzzle. And I use words like *well-being*, *mind*, *body*, *spirit*, and *wellness* because food is about more than just good nutrition. From being in the gym with clients to coaching and becoming a chef of healthy food, I have learned that in order to sustain a healthy lifestyle, you must sharpen your mind and awaken your spirit. Those play a huge overarching role in your health. I learned this through trial and error over time. Regardless of the adversity I was facing, I found a way to be the best version of myself. Taking ownership and nurturing your mind and spirit will equip you to manage your physical health.

> *"Whoever sows sparingly will also reap sparingly, and whoever sows generously will also reap generously."*
> — 2 Corinthians 9:6

Reading is a great way to sharpen the mind. We all know this, but we may be put off by the time and effort required. For the ones willing to do the work, the blessings flow. I like to use this example because it is so personal. For someone who struggled with reading as a child, to find such joy in the act of reading is amazing. I have found that through my reading about nutrition, I am able to grow, and I continue to try new things. I am outfitting my confidence with reason and knowledge. Understanding reason gives me purpose. It doesn't feel like a *do* or a *don't*—it feels like a choice.

Do you see how when we take ownership, we get to choose, but when we let someone else tell us what to do, it feels like a short-term goal with a set deadline, even a pipe dream? Learning creates the power to choose for yourself. It creates intention in our choices around what to eat, when to rest, and when to change intensity. Further along, if you trust the process, you become more intuitive.

Part of getting to know your spirit is knowing where you find peace. I like to use my husband as an example: I have been with him fifteen years, and I can easily pinpoint where he finds his peace—on the golf course. He could be hitting balls on the driving range, walking eighteen holes and carrying his bag, or driving our boys around in the golf cart, eating Goldfish crackers. He uses that time to offset the strain of growing his sales business and managing the other stresses of life. Is golf a form of exercise? Yes. Does golf require discipline? Yes. Is golf challenging? Always. Working on his game feeds his spirit. He finds his peace away from the chaos of life, where he can slow down and reset the clock. Some weeks, he's at the course three times (if he's lucky), and other weeks, he might only get to watch the Golf Channel, at night. No matter how much time he's there, it's his way of slipping away from the chaos of life to play and feed his spirit. It brings him joy.

Over the years, I have seen him improve his game and work diligently toward lowering his handicap. He keeps a sand wedge in our basement, where he chips yellow practice balls into a bucket, and sometimes at me. He has equipment he uses to practice form. He always prefers to walk the course—the way the game was intended to be played—because he is fully committed to the discipline of the practice. It's no different than me cooking to Frank Sinatra in the kitchen at home. We're both practicing fundamentals and always trying to improve. And regular practice sharpens the mind in ways that can apply to other areas of life. I like to think about this as serving oneself.

When you make time to feed your spirit, you're sustaining yourself. When you feed your spirit, you are recharging. Feeding your spirit needs to be a part of your health journey, no matter what form it takes. Two of my favorite spirit-feeding practices are cooking while listening to Frank Sinatra, and my quiet time in my office, reading and writing to strengthen my faith and root me deeper in biblical truth. Both serve my well-being and the overall picture of my journey with health.

What is your spirit-feeding practice? Do you have one? If not, why?

MY NUTRITION JOURNEY

Here's the biggest secret of all about nutrition: it's all about your mindset.

The topic of nutrition comes up differently for all of us. Some people start to think about nutrition as part of their fitness, while others may be more concerned about health conditions. Regardless of how you got to where you are today, you need to know where you want to go and what is realistic for you to manage physically *and* mentally. Both are huge components of a healthy lifestyle.

For instance, you won't be able to achieve your health and fitness goals if you're mentally prepared but not physically able to execute. In contrast, having time to work out, cook, and study nutrition (or "dieting") is great, but creating too much mental strain can be detrimental. I have experienced both situations. When I was younger, I had the time, but my obsession with looking like a fitness model led me down a mental rollercoaster. As I've matured, with a career and family, my mental state has improved, but I am challenged by time restraints. I find that if I'm not on top of my planning, I can resort to quick choices that don't align with my goals, like eating from the pantry too frequently or skipping workouts.

My journey with nutrition started at eighteen, when I got my first job as a trainer. I wanted to look fit like the models in the magazines—typical. I even started dating a bodybuilder. I was easily misled and misinformed on nutrition at an early age, and I thought the only way to get a good-looking body was to be extremely strict with my diet and not eat certain foods. This was very common for gym-goers and fitness competitors, and I wanted to look lean like them, so I adopted that diet. It led me to having an unhealthy relationship with food and my body, which consumed me for years. I constantly felt like I was being judged for what I ate. I didn't eat "bad foods" around people. I hid what I ate. I created an increasingly difficult way to live. When I would go to family functions, I couldn't enjoy the experience because I was too concerned with what not to eat, or if I should just eat everything in sight since I never allowed myself to eat those foods. The people I surrounded myself with were always talking about dieting. It was very, very different from how I was raised, and I thought they had the secret to the perfect body.

In college, I would pack a cooler with my food: a shaker bottle with two scoops of protein and one tablespoon of flaxseed oil in it (my 10:00 a.m. snack), and a Tupperware of tilapia and green beans for lunch. Since I was in between classes, I ate the fish cold, even though it meant the good fats would be coagulated at the bottom of the container, like jelly, because I was so desperate to lose weight. I used to think my suffering was making me better and healthier. I also felt like I had to stick to it if I wanted to be accepted. But I was creating mental instability with food, becoming obsessed with every choice I made. I was so worried about my image and pretending I was perfect. But I wasn't perfect. No one is. I put that pressure on myself.

After a couple of years of this, an internal voice started saying, "Jillian, this is not healthy." I wanted to change, but I felt insecure, as if people would think I was a hypocrite. I would tell my boyfriend I was going to return some movies to Blockbuster, then drive to Sonic and buy an Oreo Blast. I didn't want him to think I was cheating on my diet, and I felt ashamed I wanted ice cream when my goal was to be fit. Why would someone care that I ate one ice cream? Years of dieting and depriving myself had left me feeling desperate. I hated my body, had uncontrollable cravings, and was mentally exhausted. I knew there had to be a better way.

Balanced eating was something I'd heard about, but it sounded too easy, and the people that mentioned it didn't seem to work too hard at it; they seemed to eat what they wanted most of the time. I didn't believe that balanced eating could get me where I wanted to be. I had been brainwashed into believing that in order to lose weight, you have to diet hard and eliminate foods to get results, and that "bad foods" sabotaged my goals and should only be consumed as part of a "cheat meal." A cheat meal is where you "allow" yourself "bad foods" as occasional rewards for sticking to your diet so perfectly. If I strayed from my diet and consumed "bad foods,"

I would have to counterbalance the calories with additional exercise. It was a constant battle that was wearing on me emotionally and spiritually.

Today, I hate when people trying to lose weight use the term "cheat meal," not because it triggers me, but because I know that they are stuck in the on/off trap, and I want to help them. Everyone has to realize their own truth and choose to opt in when they are ready. You cannot force someone to opt in. It's their ownership to claim.

> *I created many false beliefs around food. Good nutrition sounded too easy and enjoyable to render results, so I fought those narratives in my head for years.*

I endeavored to take ownership of my health and learn about whole-food nutrition. It was a promise I made to myself. I wanted to have a relationship with food that didn't cause me anxiety daily. Committed to changing my relationship with food, I got certified in nutrition and continued my studies for years. (I understand this is not everyone's aspiration, but you did pick up this book. Knowledge is power!) I went on to coach and train hundreds of clients, encouraging them to take ownership of their nutrition. I got into meal prepping and taught myself how to cook and shop to support a healthy lifestyle. I learned how "macros" (macronutrients) work in the body so I could prepare balanced meals that got physical results. I made the time in my schedule to accommodate this new endeavor, all while my mental health was blossoming along with my new, healthy relationship with food.

I focused on exploring a variety of foods and different flavor profiles, trying every vegetable at the grocery store because I wanted to know about them all. These positive actions pushed me outside the box of dieting rules. I stopped obsessing about the macros on the labels and focused on where the food came from and how it was prepared. If the food was natural, the meal balanced, and the portions controlled, the macros were typically in line.

Having learned the difference between cravings and boredom, I began to honor my cravings by eating the foods I wanted. I didn't feel the need to "cheat," because if I wanted fries on a Tuesday, I just ate them with some chicken and veggies. I made it work responsibly. These practices got me closer to my ultimate goal: freedom from dieting. I didn't want food to control me anymore—but wanted to make it the vehicle that would nourish and help me.

Unfortunately, many people lack the time and/or knowledge to take ownership of their nutrition (something that is true for most of my clients/customers). I wanted to help those people, and my passion for nutrition and food led me to culinary school, where I gained professionalism in the kitchen. I was developing the concept of fit-flavors: healthy meals to go. I knew that if I understood how to properly execute cooking techniques, that would ensure a better experience for my clients, and an understanding of world culture would make for a diverse menu. If I could make the food taste better, not like the diet food people are used to, people would be more likely to adopt a healthier lifestyle (#WINNING).

The next season of my life involved learning how to manage my nutrition while facing the stress of motherhood and my career. There were some dark and challenging times that taught me valuable lessons about myself and my nutrition. During it all, I continued developing my philosophy, deeply rooted in my foundation. The information about nutrition was always there to study and implement, but in all the chaos, even I ended up seeking out fast answers through bad resources. Again, no one is perfect.

I believe everything that's happened in my life has led me to where I am now, and my experiences gave me valuable understanding of the struggles humans have around food. Now our business has the opportunity to be a resource for others. Through my personal experiences and the clients I've coached, I developed a product and concept that is sustainable and driven by results. We manage the portions and balance the macros so the consumer can just reheat and eat yummy food. The recipes I have created at home and for fit-flavors are an extension of my love and passion for food. They are pieces of my journey to nurture positive change in my mind, body, and spirit.

MY NUTRITION PHILOSOPHY

You have to be willing to learn and to identify and forfeit your false beliefs around food.

Over my almost twenty years in the fitness, culinary, and nutrition industries, I've taught fitness and nutrition to personal-training clients, large groups, customers, and even my employees. I've seen how people struggle with implementing changes in their lifestyle, with uprooting fixed mindsets around food and body image. I've seen myself struggle with the same insecurities while growing my business and having children, and I continue to learn more about how to provide the best nutrition for them. I am the happiest and healthiest I have ever been, but it's been quite the journey.

Our society faces obstacles around nutrition, including the lack of quality education on the topic. Fortunately for me, I've spent the past six years working alongside our registered dietician (RD), a licensed professional, who has taught me the psychology around how we relate to our food and helped me align our menu with nutrition and dietetics guidelines. Merriam-Webster defines *philosophy* as "a system of motivating beliefs, concepts, and principles." So a nutrition philosophy would be how one understands and relates to food and nutrition—their particular set of knowledge and personal truths about how to nourish their body. My nutrition philosophy is as follows:

- Eat whole foods as much as possible.
- Eat balanced (all macronutrients).
- Be mindful of portions.
- Love what you eat, and don't deny yourself the fun foods.
- Keep it simple.

If you read that and think it sounds too vague, no worries. I did too. Let me walk you through how I got here and why I fight so hard to facilitate this lifestyle for others.

Eat whole foods as much as possible: I mean foods that come from more natural sources—unrefined plant and animal products we keep in our refrigerators. If you think about it, God didn't intend for us to have chemicals in our foods. Many food manufacturers and chain restaurants produce low-quality products to yield high profit margins. These convenient but highly processed products—filled with sugar and white flour and laced with chemicals and preservatives—have become the norm, yet they are often detrimental to our health. The marketing on these products is designed to make you feel good about the foods you purchase, even though you may not feel the best after you eat them. Ever notice the term "whole grain" on food packaging? Sounds good, right? Well, that doesn't really mean much when there are twenty-seven grams of sugar in a single serving. Cereals are notorious for this. Slap a fun picture on there, and kids are sure to want that cereal over the box of Cheerios. And that's just one example of how these foods are affecting America's health.

Whole foods aren't always the easiest to consume (they require preparation), or even to obtain ("food deserts" are a thing), but eating them must be a priority, and understanding the marketing behind the more convenient products will help you make better choices. Fortunately, many manufacturers have found ways to produce products with minimal ingredients. And those products are readily available in so many places now. Eating whole foods is increasingly doable, even if you lead a busy life.

Eat balanced: This one takes some thought. Understanding the importance of each macronutrient is key to a balanced diet and a healthy lifestyle. Having a balanced plate means the right amount of protein, carbohydrate, and fat. Eating balanced is different for each person. Splitting up your calories into regular, smaller meals and snacks throughout your day will help you control your appetite and avoid overeating. When we eat balanced, we stabilize blood sugar levels, sustain energy, and avoid crashes. Eating stimulates our metabolism to work, and our bodies can effectively process calories (energy) if the quantity is manageable. Larger meals can make us feel tired and force the body to store what it can't use as fat. So the size of our meals is also important.

Be mindful of portions: Portion control is an amazing part of this philosophy. If you eat balanced and apply portion control, you can avoid being too rigid with your meals. It's like your meal is the bowling ball, rolling down the lane, and eating balanced and portion control are the bumpers. They keep you going in the right direction, with room on each side, but never let you fall into the gutter—or "off the wagon." With practice, you can learn to determine proper portions with your eyes and never have to use a food scale again, unless you want to. And if you manage to eat mostly real, whole food—again, in balance—you can trickle the fun stuff in where it fits. That's where the cake and tequila come in!

Love what you eat, and don't deny yourself the fun foods: Yes, you heard me right—and pizza, fries, and chocolate are also on my list. I have a theory that your healthy lifestyle should employ an 80–20 split. That's 80 percent stuff that makes you feel great and lines up with your goals and 20 percent wiggle room to enjoy the fun stuff and manage life. I've tried to find healthier substitutes for the items on my list of fun stuff, but they're often not as good as the originals, so I have the real versions sometimes but consume the substitutes more often. Getting creative with substitutes includes options like home-baked fries instead of fast-food fries, dark chocolate with nuts instead of a highly processed chocolate snack, or a slice of Whole Foods pizza topped with veggies instead of greasy takeout.

There really isn't a substitute for tequila, so I just manage it. For instance, if I'm drinking, I try to eat well and have a balanced plate—a starch, a protein, and a vegetable—keeping the bumpers on. Same with dessert; if I really want it, I don't deny myself. I either don't finish the whole thing or I share it, so it's portion controlled. I'm satisfied because I ate the real thing, but I didn't overdo it.

And if you feel compelled to eat the whole dessert every time, you are likely dealing with one of two scenarios: you're either being too restrictive, or your *why* is not clear and meaningful. If you feel guilty after eating the whole serving, you may be giving that damn treat too much power over you, so when you do have it, you feel out of control. Counterintuitively, you may need to eat smaller portions of it more often so it loses its power over you. Having a smaller serving or saying no and meaning it will come with time. It's all in your head. If you just love treats, aligning your *why* with your nutrition or wellness goal will help your choices feel more meaningful.

When I love what I'm eating and don't *deny myself* food, it never feels like a diet. Mealtime is peaceful and free of stress, at least about food. I gave up the rigid rules because they are a means to an end. Rules cause anxiety around food. And false beliefs quickly pull us back onto the hamster wheel we are trying to get off. Recognizing your triggers and false beliefs is important when changing your mindset. A well-defined *why* is crucial to building a nutrition foundation based on science and truth, to stand up to the weather of life. Life comes with stress and adversity, but if your nutrition philosophy is rooted, setbacks won't impact your health goals nearly as much.

When I was changing my mindset around food, I knew I needed to be humble and learn, that it would take time to see and feel results. I shifted my focus from weighing myself and counting carbs to eating more whole foods. I started envisioning the body I wanted and how I could get there without ditching carbs entirely. I stopped taking advice from people who were unstable with their nutrition and, instead, started learning about intuitive eating and macros. I started to eat in a way that made me feel happy. Shifting my efforts away from things that triggered me negatively and toward positive actions helped me enjoy the process. I slowly started making more changes, giving myself time to adjust. As a result, I was able to sustain the changes, and the results were astounding!

I would be lying if I told you either of my two big success stories took less than a year each. What did take less than a year was shifting my mindset. Once that was dialed in, the work needed to render the results was in full swing. Today, I am still striving to manage my healthier lifestyle amidst the challenges that life throws at me. Shifting my mindset was the differentiator. Achieving an amazing physique requires discipline in both nutrition and fitness. I have been working on both for eighteen years, and I feel like I've had the nutrition part figured out for the last twelve. Some things just start to add up over time—and you definitely have to put in the time, *period*.

THE MINDSET SHIFT

When we harness our mindset, we are strong and resilient, like a brick wall. Without that control, we are a feather in the wind.

We've all been fed up with our status quo at one point or another, and this usually leads to thoughts about what we can change. In order to make any significant lifestyle change, you have to work on your mindset. That's not something you can get at most gyms. It's not easy and you can't buy it. And only the people who have gone deep and come out the other side can really explain it.

You might be wondering, *How is changing how I think going to help me lose weight or get fit? I need to lose [X] pounds!* Let me remind you that your mindset around how you attack your goals is a primary reason why you struggle, why you can't maintain results. It's your perspective on your approach. This is where the power of mindset comes in. If we are constantly trying to achieve what is not sustainable, we are lying to ourselves and not taking ownership of the real work we need to do. That may not be what you want to hear, but I don't support any of the quick, trendy ways of losing weight in the short term.

If you ask anyone who has achieved a healthy lifestyle—who is visibly happy and makes everything look easy—they'll tell you it's about perspective and consistency. And they'll tell you there is no set start or end point—just life and the pursuit of well-being. The more disciplined you are, the faster you start seeing the change play out. But you have to go at your own pace, and you have to own your mindset. Because if you rely too much on someone else to get you there—therapist, trainer, personal chef, coach, mentor, etc.—you might as well be on your own. Other people can coach you and hold you accountable, which I love, but you have to fully own what you are manifesting. This is 100 percent your responsibility, and if you are dedicated enough to the pursuit, you will succeed. It comes down to the effort you apply and the space you make available for your mind to sharpen and for new habits to develop.

(WARNING: Be wary of advice from people who look amazing during certain seasons but are on a different diet each year. It's not just the diet you follow or how many calories you burn—it's the relationship you have with food and your body *and* that you want to keep honoring yourself.)

Have you ever felt fear surrounding a belief that you were so sure was true? Moving past such a belief requires looking beyond your current awareness to understanding a new, outside perspective. It's like you need to completely erase what you know and start over to change your beliefs, if that is your goal. Consider politics, for example: in order for someone to understand an opposing viewpoint, they have to humble themselves so they can open their mind, listen, and learn. They need to set aside their limiting beliefs and open themselves to a larger view.

It won't be easy; you'll have to give stuff up, change your environment, and get used to saying no as well as explaining yourself to people. If it were easy to do, everyone would have their shit together and be living their dreams. The reality is, however, that most people are not humble enough to let go of their beliefs. They're not willing to ask for help (perhaps out of pride). And they're not willing to do the deep work on themselves. That's a hurdle you'll have to get over if you want to learn and grow. (I believe that God has his hand in this. I'm serious—each time I've harnessed the power of my spirituality, my perspective has broadened, and the possibilities have opened up.)

Along your indefinite journey toward well-being, you'll likely face setbacks, and that can be disheartening. Unfortunately, failure and disappointment can cut deep, affecting more than just your physical body and emotions. Failure affects your spirit. The less connected you are with your spirit, the less self-aware you are, and that makes it harder to rebound from disappointment and failure. Your spirit is what allows you to look inward. It's your relationship with yourself and what connects you to God. Spirituality involves a deeper connection to your well-being that will serve you on any journey you face, including pursuing a healthier lifestyle.

Despite any physical or emotional challenges, know that you have the power to harness your spirit to work on a much deeper level.

To harness the power of your spirit, you must look inward and know what you want. For example, I harnessed this power to shift my career and my nutrition. When I lost my business, I had to defeat anxiety and put my ego in check to start over with a clear vision. With my nutrition, I was tired of dieting and wanted to improve my relationship with food, so I had to change my approach. Both times, I had to look deeper to resolve the root issue.

To this day, I still struggle with my mindset around not feeling smart enough. That fear has been rooted in my head since I was a child. When I was in elementary school, I struggled with reading. I specifically remember sitting on the colorful carpet in Mrs. Trackslor's first-grade classroom and being asked to make the sounds of the letters on the flash card she held up. For some reason, when the "horn" card was flashed and I was supposed to make an *H* sound, I couldn't do it. I was six years old, and my classmates were staring at me—I felt anxious. I felt that way every time we worked on reading.

Eventually, I was called to leave class in the middle of the day to go work with a tutor, along with two other students, and we continued doing this for a time. Every time we got up to leave for tutoring, kids would smirk and giggle. I felt ashamed. I remember my mom sending me to Sylvan Learning Center. Sitting in front of a computer, I was prompted to practice fundamentals such as pronouncing my long and short vowels. While I got more one-on-one attention, I didn't feel any less ashamed, nor did I learn any faster. I ended up getting a D in reading that year. I felt like a failure. I associated that D with my inability to learn and grow. And I let that define me—I believed it. And I carried that belief throughout school. Those early experiences have haunted me into my adult years, continuing to shape my mindset around learning. Eventually, I realized I have an easier time comprehending reading I actually enjoy (duh!).

When I ventured into business, I still believed I wasn't smart enough. What I failed to realize at the time was that I had a fixed mindset around my learning and comprehension. Just because I was behind the curve in reading comprehension and grammar didn't mean I couldn't lead a company— though I did rely heavily on spell-check (and still do). Instead of letting my weaknesses hold me back, I leaned on others for help when necessary—allowing me to focus more on my strengths. I recognized that my fixed mindset around being or feeling smart wasn't serving me—in life or in business—so I shifted my perspective.

As I said, I also used to have a fixed mindset around nutrition. False narratives entered my head early on; I was the weak sheep marketers and diet "experts" prey on. And not being educated on the topic only made things worse—a recipe for disaster. Because I was trying to meet someone else's unrealistic and unsustainable expectations, I was living in fear and making decisions that didn't serve my well-being. The goals I set were shortsighted and required eliminating something in the pursuit of losing weight. Living that way is like living in a small box—you can't stretch out or relax.

Learning to eat healthy and serve your nutrition goals is

like sailing: Would you try to sail a boat if you didn't know the safety rules? What about the complexities of the wind, water, and sails? What about navigation? What if you fall overboard? If you don't learn the ropes (pun intended), you're just a person on a boat that probably won't sail far. Even if you improvise, managing to cast off and catch some wind, you can only fake it for so long before you inevitably make a critical mistake or just want to give up out of frustration. But if you learn the interplay between the wind, the water, the sails, and the rest of the boat, and if you know how to figure out where you want to go, you'll have everything you need to get there. So if you want to sail farther than the dock and enjoy the trip, you need to open yourself to learning and growing as a sailor.

The same goes for food: if you don't learn how to "navigate" nutrition, how do you expect to know how to eat right? Eating balanced—smooth sailing—requires some training. You need to shift your mindset and learn how to sail your own nutrition boat, so to speak, or you'll probably just drift aimlessly or end up riding on someone else's (#LOSING).

When working to shift your mindset, self-awareness is crucial, as being blind to the truths of your circumstances and behaviors will hold you back. Things you do, say, and/or believe may not be serving you. You will have to attack those unhealthy behaviors head-on. Unfortunately, your current mindset may resist. And it is possible to have a fixed mindset in one area but a growth mindset in another area. Overall, shifting any mindset requires changing narratives and wrestling with your deepest beliefs, which is a process in itself, but it is essential to finding the confidence you seek.

Another way to tackle your mindset is to be practical and resourceful. That means focusing on your strengths while seeking out people and other resources to help in areas you aren't as strong. This "go where you flow" approach is common among the entrepreneurs I've met. I tend to excel at learning and comprehension in the areas that interest me, those that I want to grow in. That I wrote this book is surprising given my past belief that I wasn't smart. I used to think only smart people write books. But the reality is that anyone who can get their shit together, tell a compelling story, add value, and get over their fear can write a book.

Again, the kind of shift we're talking about is going to require a commitment to a lot of work over a long period of time. Changing your lifestyle is not achieved by just saying what you want to do, talking about it for a bit, and then working a little harder. And challenging old beliefs in order to grow is a big job, but you have your whole life ahead of you to practice harnessing its power. Do it once, and you can do it again. Do it again, and maybe you can help others do it. (Big secret: I didn't do it by myself. I asked God to step in.)

This book is just a tool in the process, a guide to help you get going in the right direction. It'll all start coming to fruition when you make the space for the growth you are looking to experience—in your nutrition, fitness, or anything else, for that matter. But one thing at a time, right? To that effect, the last seven chapters of this book will cover actionable themes you can tackle at your own pace:

1. Visualization
2. Speaking new narratives
3. Writing
4. Education
5. Making time
6. Owning and processing the failures
7. Trusting the process

Are you ready?

VISUALIZATION

Visualization can be done anywhere and for anything. Sometimes it feels weird, and you might even feel guilty, like you don't deserve the outcome you envision. Do it anyway. Be specific and play the story out in your head. There is no right answer—it is your creation.

We just talked about the importance of shifting your mindset when pursuing a healthier lifestyle, and coming to terms with the work required is part of the process. If that seems daunting, maybe you need a clearer picture of your desired results to help start the shift.

Visualization is more than just pictures—it's how you want to look and feel, how you want to spend your time, who you want to spend it with, how you want to live your life. Visualizing these kinds of details plays a strong role in developing your mind to work for you, not against you.

The first step in working toward the life you want is visualizing it in detail—your routine, the clothes you wear, the food you eat, how you feel, who you are with, etc. You have to dream a little, even if you don't think or believe it's possible. You must visualize what you want in order to understand the work involved and embrace it. While you are lying in bed, or while you're stuck in traffic, imagine the life you want to create and how happy you will be when you get there. This simple visualization exercise starts a little fire in your subconscious mind, which you can feed to help fuel your future reality. Even more powerful, write it down; describe or make a list of the results you want to see or the goals you want to achieve.

Note: If this process does not excite you, you might not be clear on *why* you want to make a lifestyle change in the first place. And if you have no idea why you are motivated to change, how do you expect to hold yourself accountable as you work toward your goal? Consider addressing your *why* first.

I'm sure you've heard of a "vision board," a piece of cardstock or cardboard covered in aspirational imagery—drawings, cut-out images from magazines, powerful phrases, etc.—which you hang somewhere you'll see it daily, maybe even set as your desktop background. The thought is that the more you visualize living that life, the more likely you are to manifest it. This practice resonates with some people, but you do not have to make one. At its core, visualization is mostly about playing out scenarios.

I created a vision board years ago, and it's still in my bathroom. One of the pictures on it is of two cute bikini-clad ladies sitting in lawn chairs, laughing, both with great hair. For me, that image represents the happy life I want—comfortable in my own skin, laughing with friends, on a vacation I earned by working hard, and great hair because that's important to me. That picture is powerful because it is what I want to become, and it reminds me why I eat well, exercise, call my friends, and take care of my hair. Today, I have a girlfriend I travel with multiple times a year, and we are often laughing in our bikinis and eating guacamole together on a beach. That vision has come to fruition.

Another image on my vision board is of a huge refrigerator with a clear glass door. Through the glass, you can see perfectly stacked containers of different foods, neat rows of several different drinks with labels facing out, and fresh fruits and veggies displayed in the bottom drawers. It is really the only material thing I have ever truly wanted, more than any car or piece of jewelry. To me, that fridge says, "You have to work hard to afford me. When you get me, you will keep me clean and organized, because I'll hold all the food that supports your healthy lifestyle as well as all the entertaining you want to do out of your new kitchen." I have been visualizing that fridge for the past ten years—I smile every time I see it. Next to the überfridge is a picture of four stacked food containers full of precut fruits and veggies, ready to eat or use in cooking. That picture is important to me because I know I'll be responsible for keeping those things in the fridge. I am preparing myself for the future I am creating.

Even before I had kids, I always envisioned having a family that sat down and ate meals together as well as being someone who taught my kids about nutrition—not by talking about it but by serving the kinds of balanced meals that support a healthy lifestyle. I imagine my hungry teenage boys coming home from school or practice and raiding the kitchen as they toss a football back and forth. I imagine them having their hungry friends over for dinner or for parties, because our house would be a fun place to hang out. I see a huge new center island full of snacks to feed a hungry crowd of guests. I see myself working hard to provide those valuable experiences and model good habits for my children and their friends. I see happy faces and healthy kids. My boys are currently only five and seven, so their teen years are still a ways off, and I've hosted large groups of adults and kids before, but I can see so clearly—in detail—the future I want to create for my children. I want it so badly. And continually visualizing this future down to the tiniest details keeps me focused on bringing it to fruition. When I work to create that future—with my vision clear and my mindset primed—it doesn't feel like work. I see it as taking one step closer to what I want. Do you see the shift in perspective?

I remember being so sick and tired of feeling bad, being restrictive, and not having the body I wanted. When I first tried to visualize my new life in which I would have a healthy and happy relationship with food, it was harder to see because I had so many established habits and beliefs that were not serving me. Seeing others that seemed happy gave me hope, but I thought it odd they didn't seem to be trying all that hard, which really got to me at the time. Regardless, I started visualizing the specifics of my new life: the waistline I wanted to have, the clothes I wanted to feel confident wearing, the variety of delicious foods I saw myself enjoying at restaurants. I saw myself enjoying sweets and desserts but not eating as much or finishing entire servings, because I wanted to feel in control and at peace. I envisioned a lot of these things to help paint the picture of what I was going to work hard to create in my life.

Having come out the other side of that struggle, I now know that it's not that they weren't working hard—but that their hard work felt more meaningful and enjoyable. It doesn't feel like life or death if I miss something. I enjoy the way I feel. And understandably, it can be harder to flip that switch in your brain and see your ideal future if your present kind of sucks and you don't feel good. You might have a vague desire to lose weight or get fit but lack the motivation to exercise, cook, or even get up off the couch. If that's where you are, the truth is that you most likely won't achieve much—unless you define your vision of success. Getting clear on what you want to accomplish is one small, simple step in the right direction, and that's how all intentional growth starts. Cooking and exercising can come later. Just start with something small.

Much like keeping a positive mindset, visualization isn't a one-day activity. I still envision the healthy life I want to have. I regularly visualize myself in a beach house with a big heated sunroom, where I'm doing yoga and getting my daily sweat in, the beach stretching out in front of me. I see myself sitting on the deck, reading and watching the sun rise over the ocean. I picture my kids being there when they are older, all of us going out to dinner. I see myself playing golf or just staying in for some quiet time with God. I'm probably retired. Sometimes I feel guilty for sharing my visualizations, but they are mine, and I've been able to make many of them happen. Dream big!

Below are some probing questions to help you get clear on the healthy lifestyle you envision, specifically regarding food. You may not have clear answers to each, but the questions that resonate with you tell you where you might want to start making some changes. As you answer, replace anything you realize you *don't* want with something you *do* want.

1. What does the phrase "relationship with food" mean to you?
2. What is your relationship with food? Can you give examples of how you eat when you go out?
3. What do you do when you are unprepared for something? How do you feel after you try to do that thing anyway?
4. Do you hold strong beliefs about nutrition? If so, what are they?
5. Do you feel trapped by a belief about certain foods, food groups or categories, macronutrients, or types of diets and how they work? If so, is that belief based on scientific fact, or just something you heard?
6. What rigid rules or guidelines do you follow in regard to food? Why do you follow them?
7. Are you open to a completely different way of thinking about what you know?
8. How does it make you feel when you are hungry but unprepared for a meal? What do you do? Do you feel confident in your food choices?

9. Do you feel like you are too rigid with nutrition guidelines?

10. Are you constantly ready to jump on anything that might get you closer to your goal? What was the latest thing you committed to?

11. Are you "on" something or "doing" something—a diet, a fad, a regimen, etc.? Why?

12. If you've set a goal, why is that goal so important to you? In what ways will you feel fulfilled when you reach it?

13. Is your relationship with food causing you to struggle in other areas of your life?

14. Are you sick and tired of feeling or eating the way you do?

15. Are you confused about how nutrition works?

16. What do you need to learn before you can confidently make better food decisions?

17. What would your typical day look like if you were living a healthy lifestyle? What would you be eating? What would you be doing differently?

Again, use whichever question (or questions) struck a chord in you. Build on that. Start to see things the way you want. (You could also easily modify the questions above to help you gain perspective on other areas of your life—fitness, career, relationships, etc.)

Another exercise that can help you visualize your new healthy life is to imagine your perfect day—actually make an itinerary. What would a perfect day look like for you, honoring your health and well-being? Lay it out. As an example, here is mine:

5:30 a.m.	Wake up; coffee/tea and supplements
5:40 a.m.	Spiritual growth time—walk, read, jounal, be with God, or work out
7:15 a.m.	Breakfast with family—I am present!
8:30 a.m.	Leave for work
10:30 a.m.	Snack
1:00 p.m.	Lunch: fit-flavors meal or quick and balanced plate
3:00 p.m.	Grab-and-go snack and afternoon tea
4:30 p.m.	Pick up kids—be present with them (electronics off)
5:00 p.m.	Make and eat dinner with family
6:00 p.m.	Playtime with my boys
8:00 p.m.	Put kids to bed; back to work for a bit
9:00 p.m.	Quality time with Jason; bedtime snack
10:00 p.m.	Bedtime

#WINNING

Obviously, life is chaotic, and things won't always go as planned, but that's why this is just an exercise. With your ideal day detailed out, you can make small decisions that get you a bit closer to living the lifestyle you want. Now, I bet it would make you feel better to see what one of my crazy days looks like. Here you go:

6:15 a.m.	Wake up (late); coffee/tea; forget to take supplements
6:25 a.m.	Computer work and emails
7:00 a.m.	Miss/skip breakfast in rush to get ready
8:00 a.m.	Scheduled appointment—don't feel grounded
9:15 a.m.	Arrive at work (late), my mind scattered
10:30 a.m.	Grab a fit-flavors meal
2:00 p.m.	Eat another fit-flavors meal
5:15 p.m.	Get home (late); nothing planned for dinner; kids want buttered pasta— I eat whatever
9:00 p.m.	Put kids to bed (late); feel guilty; handle loose ends with work/housework; feel general anxiety
10:00 p.m.	Late snack
11:00 p.m.	Go to bed (late), completely exhausted
#LOSING	

As I visualize my goal and work on my self-discipline, I create more and more boundaries around my time and my appointments. This keeps some structure in my day to allow for my daily practice while prioritizing my health and well-being. If I am not working one day, I may get a facial or a massage or take a personal appointment. I typically spend one or two hours of my day taking care of myself. Yes, it is selfish—but I wouldn't change it for the world. I worked to create this life. If I am going to sustain and maintain a happy, healthy, sexy Jillian, I need my girl time, and nobody can argue with that. I find and make the time to do more. You can too.

SPEAKING NEW NARRATIVES

"It's the repetition of affirmations that leads to belief. And once that belief becomes a deep conviction, things begin to happen."
— Muhammad Ali

Have you ever experienced anxiety or fear in regard to losing weight, counting calories or macronutrients, meal times, dieting for a trip, or labeling foods "good" or "bad"? If any of these things consume your mind, recognize they will most likely be a trigger for a while. Being "triggered" means having an emotional or physical reaction to a previous trauma.

I was triggered by net carbs and sugar-free foods for a long time. Avoiding sugar and minimizing carbs went hand in hand. To avoid eating sugar, I abused artificially sweetened foods. For instance, if something was "sugar free," I thought that meant it was healthy to eat and would help me be healthy. The (anxious) narrative in my head went something like this:

> *Low-carb diets make you lose weight. Sugar is a bad carb. Don't eat sugar if you want to lose weight. Fruit is bad because it has sugar. You can't eat bananas and grapes if you want to lose weight. Sugar-free foods are foods that are sweet with no real carbs. Eat sugar-free foods to help you lose weight . . .*

That extremely restrictive narrative was the result of listening to the wrong advice, my lack of education, and my desperate desire to quickly lose weight. And I held on to it for way too long.

In reality, sugar-free foods are laced with artificial ingredients that can cause bloating. And when you eat artificially sweetened foods, your body believes it is going to receive actual sugar; when that doesn't happen, well, you crave sugar even more. I've also read studies about how people who drink diet soda are more likely to be overweight than those who don't drink it at all, not to mention that artificial sweeteners are highly addictive. Looking back, I'm not sure why the hell I didn't research this stuff. I guess I just wanted to look like the people I saw that supposedly ate that way all the time. And that is a thought pattern of someone who is not taking ownership of their nutrition.

When I was eating that way, I constantly felt deprived. I used to chew a pack of gum a day just because I craved sweetness. To combat that trigger, I sought out nutrient-dense foods—reading all the ingredients, instead of just the macros. Trusting that new process was hard because my false narratives told me it would make me gain more weight. The research on this topic says just the opposite. Everything I read about healthy nutrition contradicted my false narratives. Once I learned the science—once I knew what was *real*—I felt less like a victim to the false narratives I was running. I still felt triggered all the time, but I had the knowledge necessary to start writing new narratives.

Here is a more comprehensive list of the *false* beliefs that held me back for years:

- I believed meals needed to be spaced three hours apart for optimal results, and that any other frequency was detrimental.
- I believed carbohydrates eaten late at night could not be used for energy and would instead be converted into fat, because activity goes down at night.
- I believed the only appropriate time to eat anything sweet was after working out, when glycogen stores are depleted and need refilling.
- I believed sugar-free foods were a good substitute for calorie-dense choices, thinking that "sugar free" meant "less calories."
- I believed egg whites were better than whole eggs because all the fat is in the yolk.
- I believed gaining muscle required eating an *insane* amount of protein.

- I believed fruit contained way too much sugar to be a healthy food.
- I believed the only way to burn fat was by taking fat-burning supplements and doing cardio at certain times of the day.
- I believed eating sugar alcohol prevented consumed carbs from turning into fat.
- I believed having a "cheat meal" meant I could eat whatever and however much I wanted.
- I believed veggies such as carrots and peas were too sugary and starchy to be considered "good."

I also compared myself to other women—regardless of age or how long they had been working on themselves, physically or mentally—solely based on their physical appearance at the time. And despite thinking I was doing the right things, I was frequently inflamed, bloated, tired, hungry, and craving sweets, plus my body fat was 10 percent higher than it is today. I was unhappy with food in many ways. What false narrative around nutrition do you tell yourself? Can you see how they play out in your life? Can you see how we can run false narratives about practically anything (food, success, relationships, etc.)?

When life throws me a tough situation, it's hard to stay positive. Our nature is to want to give up or find the easy way. It's not easy to do what is hard or right. Your narratives are weapons—they can be used *against* you or used *by* you. No one is going to monitor the voices in your head or make sure you are using positive self-talk except for you and maybe your therapist. So keep your "weapons" sharp and pointed in the right direction.

WRITING

Writing has been an expression of frustration, love, gratitude, and learning for me. I never wrote before I lost my first business. Writing helped heal me, get my goals on paper, and realize my progress.

When I got serious about changing my perspective around food, I let go of the restrictive thinking around numbers and elimination and shifted my focus to positive actions, such as eating more veggies and making sure my plate looked fairly balanced. I love to post on social media about "eating the rainbow." But that only makes up a small portion of my writing. I used to have tons of paper journals lying around, but today I mostly write at my computer. I write about everything from prayers to frustrations, gratitude, and lessons—whatever internal stuff I want to express or process externally. Writing can be a powerful tool when enacting change in your life.

Visualization and challenging false narratives are only boosted when you give them tangible form, whether on paper or a screen. In the previous chapter, I asked you to bring consciousness to the negative, and in this chapter, I'll ask you to replace the negatives with positives—to focus on affirmations. Affirmations are *positive* propositions, statements, or judgments. By saying or writing them, you are affirming them to be true (even if you don't yet believe them). This is also called "positive self-talk." This is huge if you plan to sustain something; otherwise, you will be miserable in the process.

> *I signed the lease yesterday, and that was exciting. I feel as if we are getting closer and closer. I do not want to do this without you. Lord, guide Jason and I where we need to go with this equipment lease and the direction of the store. I have faith that if I stay open to the plan you have for my life, I will go in the right direction. I am open to your guidance.*
> *— Journal entry, April 9, 2013*

You may have heard some iteration of "Read it, write it, know it, say it, believe it, become it." The reason that advice is popular is because that is how most of us learn best.

Following up your reading or thinking with writing activates the information. It's powerful! If you skip this step and just read the rest of this book, you won't get the full benefit of this process. You'd be rushing—not the right mindset to support real change. I constantly talk about the work involved in creating change, and writing is part of that work. Writing turns the internal into the external—you can better see it, confront it, and process it. Do it, and come back to it later to reflect on your progress.

Below, you'll find a list of my affirmations from when I was shifting my own mindset. They are less about my physical body and more about my thought process and overall mindset. Don't get this confused with the loving self-talk you might employ to combat not being happy with your physical appearance. Losing weight and keeping it off is a big deal, but you need to support that effort with the right mindset. And affirmations provide support, but they won't get you results—that's what work and focus are for. Start with the mindset, and the physical will follow.

As you read my affirmations, notice how they start with "I will," marking my intent to follow through on my goals, which supports my shift in thinking. As I remind myself of these affirmations, saying "I will . . ." out loud helps me stay focused on my goals.

- I will stop thinking so much about numbers and being perfect and instead focus on quality, portion control, and balance—reducing my anxiety and promoting a sustainable lifestyle.

- I will eat fruit every day and understand the value it provides my body, so I won't be scared to eat it and can have a well-balanced diet—because I love fruit!

- I will allow myself to go out to eat with family and friends without feeling guilty about the food I order, because one meal out shouldn't "ruin" my new lifestyle. I can make any menu work as long as I focus on creating a balanced plate that is portion controlled.

- I will find a way to eat from all food groups throughout the day, even if I stray from my plan, which is likely. I should be able to shift on the fly without feeling stressed.

- I will stop saying "bad food" and will instead refer to it as "fun food." "Bad food" sounds negative, whereas "fun food" sounds positive—plus I love french fries!

- I will learn how to incorporate fun foods into my nutrition responsibly, without hindering my physical goals.

- I will indulge in fun foods responsibly and not feel guilty afterward.

- I will not guilt myself into exercise because of a food decision, instead reflecting on why I ate it and becoming more mindful of my food choices.

- I will educate myself about the science of macros so I'm not intimidated by them.

- I will strive to eat nutrient-dense foods instead of ones marketed as "low sugar," "low carb," or "low calorie."

- I will stop weighing myself every day, because the number consumes me and doesn't help my mindset.

- I will become more intuitive about what my body needs and be receptive to its hunger cues.

- I will not be distracted from my goals by friends or influencers evangelizing their routines, diet regimens, or opinions. This is *my* journey, and I'm taking full ownership no matter how long it takes.

- I will learn to live this way without draining my energy. It will feel so natural, I won't even think about it anymore.

(That last affirmation is the pinnacle of my lifestyle goals. I'm there now, but it took about five years.) I didn't just sit down one day and write that entire list; it came together over time as I caught myself in negative narratives I wanted to release.

Go ahead and write down some affirmations of your own. If you can't list everything today, no worries; keep the list in your pocket, purse, or journal so you can add to it as more things come up. You can refer back to it often, reminding yourself of the narratives you want to change. Once you have identified your negative narratives and reframed them as affirmations, start working on them. This will require making adjustments to your daily life.

This is where the work comes in. Affirmations alone are not going to get your results. But you do get to decide what constitutes "results." For me, it meant making time to learn, read, cook, and plan more. I had a lot of bad habits to break and a lot of new habits to adopt. Implementing even one new habit is hard; you have to be consistent for months before your brain correlates that habit as a natural process. That is why an "all or nothing" mentality doesn't work; if you start a completely different schedule all at once, you can easily be thrown off or discouraged by the first challenge you encounter. I do know a small handful of people with extremely regimented schedules and lifestyles—they don't go out much. And if that works for them, more power to them. They probably aren't reading this book. In my opinion, real life requires "wiggle room." Changing habits takes time, so remember to show yourself grace in the process.

Every attempt you make at trying something new is a step in the right direction. Not everything you try will flow with your new lifestyle, but you need to keep trying things until you find what works for you. For inspiration, here are some examples of small changes you could make—start with one—to support a healthier lifestyle:

- If you want to start having smoothies with breakfast but find the prep and cleanup discouraging, find a different solution or find shortcuts to make the smoothie less daunting (e.g., buying smoothies; making a few days' worth at a time).

- If you want to start cooking more, be realistic with yourself. Maybe aim to cook one or two nights a week for starters, and be consistent for a few months, until it feels easier.

- Find a few quick, go-to meals or snacks that take less than three to five minutes to prepare, and consider making them in bulk to cover a few days, if practical.

- If you want to start exercising, start small, but be consistent. If you need inspiration, consider a trainer or a class, but don't miss sessions—put them on your schedule. (Don't forget to account for the time you need to drive and shower as well as what you will need to give up.) If it feels like more hassle than it's worth, you either need to find a more convenient solution or find a different type of exercise that you will enjoy making time for—walking, biking, sports, etc.

- In general, if you want to get serious about changing your life, work on one area of your life at a time, and be consistent with it for months before you try to change much else. And never try to change everything at once.

If something doesn't work for you, keep trying things until you find what does. Once you find what works for you—what starts to feel easier to do on a regular basis—that means you have made space for it. And keeping it on your schedule will only help you maintain the habit. But that doesn't mean you have to stop there. A habit of going on a morning walk could turn into going to a morning workout class. Cooking dinner at home one night a week could turn into cooking multiple nights a week, because you understand the time commitment. And so on. Stopping bad habits frees up bandwidth to start good habits, and you can gradually build momentum, introducing more and more change at your own pace.

This is why you can't compare yourself to others, especially people who are further along with health and nutrition. Odds are they have been working at it for years. Also, never compare yourself to other people, especially if they have a different family dynamic than you—raising kids is a job in itself. If you do have kids or your circumstances limit how much time you can spend on yourself, consider seeking outside help—child care, food delivery, etc. Whatever it takes to free up even a small amount of time is probably worth it to allow you to work on yourself. Today, on top of running my business and being a mom, I have three to four workouts scheduled a week, and I order fit-flavors meals to save time. I can keep up with my workouts, and dinner is ready when I am. I prefer to cook, but having a busy life means that isn't always possible.

Writing brings more intention to your visual and narrative mind. It is a way to invest in yourself. No one else is going to know that you did it (unless you tell them), but I promise you won't regret it. It might feel weird at times, but that's normal, so do it anyway—as often as you want or need to.

EDUCATION

Being motivated to change is being willing to learn.

For years, I thought I could follow a different trendy diet approach to lose extra weight. I just kept thinking that the answer was out there—something I hadn't yet tried. Being uneducated on proper nutrition left me hanging on to whatever sounded hopeful. I still encounter this warped mindset in people I meet, even my own customers.

I've been told that our meals supposedly contain "too many carbs," but the people that say that don't seem to understand what carbs do or how many they should be consuming to reach their goals. They've just latched on to the low-carb craze because the people they listen to who lose weight talk about that. Or they will ask me how many calories they should be eating, like I should know. I don't know anything about them, so why would they trust me to answer that question without all relevant information? That uneducated approach leads to a dead end, but it doesn't have to be that way. You can be free of the unhealthy narratives by educating yourself and managing your 80–20.

Even now, as a chef, I like to look back and appreciate how far I have come. Being able to reflect and laugh at yourself—to find the humor in past decisions, e.g., how you used to dress, do your hair, etc.—is a sign of personal growth. Here's a favorite story of mine about how bad I used to be at cooking:

When Jason and I started living together, I was an aspiring chef, so we decided to invest in some nice cooking appliances—a new fridge, stove, and microwave—as well as new countertops and backsplashes. I remember picking out the backsplashes and him doing the installation—it was so special. The first day our home was clear of construction dust, I decided to hard-boil some eggs on the stove top. Basic stuff, right? When I cracked them open, I noticed they were nowhere near done. I had already dumped the water and was left with six undercooked, mostly raw eggs. Too impatient to wait for water to boil on the stove again, I decided to just microwave the remaining in-shell eggs in a bowl of water, because that would do the trick . . . right? Three minutes later, lo and behold, the second I opened the door, a hot egg bomb went off in my face, splattering hot egg pieces all over me and the kitchen, even the ceiling—a literal "hot mess." I spent the next thirty minutes being pissed about my eggs, bummed about my kitchen mess, and disappointed in myself for thinking I could microwave eggs in their shells. Who does that? (Young me, apparently.) A week later, I found my cat playing with a yellow ball in the living room—a cooked yolk. I guess that one got away. And that story is just one example.

Yeah, so when I first got into cooking, I really didn't know what I was doing. I was awful, to say the least. But I wanted to learn to cook so I could manage my new, healthy lifestyle—so I could own it. And when I took ownership of learning how food works in the body, it freed me from gimmicky promises, weight-loss programs that eliminated food groups, and comparing myself to fitness models. I could let go of the lies because my learning led to understanding. (Also, I later learned that most of the women I desired to look like only looked that way for a short period of time and most likely dieted hard leading up to their photoshoots.) It turned out that the "it" thing I was missing was knowledge. And a great thing about learning is that it requires us to break old habits and false narratives. It helps us rewire our instincts and see the world from a new perspective, which can ultimately serve us in creating new habits.

I knew that getting to where I wanted to be would take a lot of work. Fortunately, studying nutrition was fun for me, as I was pumped to start my new endeavors and live my new narratives. Plus, I knew the research and learning would ultimately serve my health. No longer would I rely on other people, marketing, or magazines to supply all my information. I still relied on other people for support, but I was sailing my own boat. Sure, it was scary—but also liberating! Once I was in chef school, learning cooking techniques, I already knew how to build a balanced plate and how to create a flavor profile. The more I learned, the more empowered I felt around food. It's a great feeling!

Today, I am a trained chef, and I love cooking! But you don't need to train as a chef to learn about food, nutrition, and cooking. Little by little over time, as you learn and practice, you will become what you desire if you put in the work. Fortunately for me, it was something I was passionate about. I understand that many people don't enjoy or want to cook, and that's why there are meal-prep companies, Pinterest recipes, and grab-and-go options at stores. Focus on the education part, and do your best to find food solutions that work best for you.

I encourage you to learn why you are eating the way you are. If your program or process feels restricted or has harsh rules, know why. Are you on a short weight-loss program? If so, what's your plan once it's over? Do you have education around how to maintain your results following the program? Is the program teaching you, or just holding you accountable? Is it teaching you good practices that you enjoy and can sustain, or is it creating more anxiety? Are you eliminating foods for your health, or to lose weight? These are all good questions to answer with confidence. And don't lie to yourself; if you don't know, own it. I let my ego suppress my need for education for years. Don't let your ego do that to you.

Obviously, everyone's needs are different. If you have food allergies or certain health conditions, education is not only even more important but entirely necessary in helping you adapt and achieve your best health. Someone reducing or eliminating carbs from their diet to lose weight, for example, is much different from a diabetic person having to manage their insulin, including learning about carb control and carb cycling. Similarly, someone eliminating gluten from their diet to lose weight is different from someone with an autoimmune disease, such as celiac, avoiding gluten because it causes debilitating symptoms.

Learning about your own body is just another part of your relationship with food. If you have health concerns related to food, you should definitely speak to a doctor or a registered dietitian (RD) to learn what foods you should and shouldn't eat because of your circumstances. An RD is an expert in nutrition as it relates to disease. They identify and treat disease-related states and conduct medical nutrition therapy, including talking about many of the psychological aspects of our relationship with food.

You might also benefit from learning directly from someone who exemplifies the healthy habits you want to foster. When I speak to individuals regarding nutrition, I can quickly determine if they are experts in their field or simply trapped in a narrative—which comes with practice. Taking advice from other people is scary when you don't know much yourself, so starting with reputable, credentialed sources is the way to go.

Wouldn't we all feel more confident with nutrition and food if we knew why the heck we were eating this or that? Today at fit-flavors, it's our mission to be the best resource for the communities we serve, providing both food and education. There's just so much BS out there that takes advantage of people's insecurities and/or lack of knowledge. Education is key to building confidence around making your own decisions. The sooner you take ownership of your nutrition and learn about your body, the sooner you'll start building a solid foundation.

MAKING TIME

Showing grace is a commitment to consistency and the end goal, not perfection.

When I started culinary school, I had just started meal prepping on the weekends to launch fit-flavors. I was still working thirty hours a week as a personal trainer, going to night classes twenty hours a week, and doing personal cheffing Fridays through Sundays—around one hundred hours of work every week. There were no days off, and I was tired all the time, pretty much living on energy drinks. Launching a business, working to pay bills, and going to school were my priorities—the things I made time to do no matter what.

I remember feeling bad about what I saw as failures: gaining weight, my body composition changing, eating unbalanced, etc. I tried to work out twice during the week—I worked at a gym, for goodness' sake—but I was so tired that it never felt good. And I was so hyped up on my new business that I didn't prioritize working out on the weekends either. That's not to say that eating balanced and exercising weren't on my mind. I could have trained fewer clients. I could have turned down new clients to cook for. Hell, I could have not gone to school. But I'd prioritized those items to level up in my career, knowing that I could, and would, get my fitness back to where I wanted it to be once my schooling was complete. That was the first time in my life that I showed myself grace for the hurdles I was facing. I was early in my nutrition journey, so I'd yet to establish the good habits I have now. I probably would have had a slightly easier time with my busy schedule if I'd established better foundational habits earlier, but such is life—live and learn.

Another time in my life where finding time was nearly impossible was when I had just opened a third fit-flavors location. Vincent, our one-year-old, was co-sleeping with Jason and me, waking us up multiple times throughout the night, and Salvatore, our six-month-old, was sleeping in a basinet, needing breastfeeding two to three times a night. We didn't sleep through the night for two years. And at work, we'd gone from twenty to forty-five employees overnight. And the company was growing so fast that I lost control of culture, training, processes and procedures, food costing, and labor management. On the opening day of our third location, I had a mental breakdown and hid in the office, crying. I needed to change how I was doing things, and I needed help.

I decided to invest in myself personally and professionally and do some hardcore personal development. There was extra time somewhere, and I was committed to finding it. I got more disciplined and structured with my schedule, such as waking up earlier to have quiet time with God as well as work on my business and my sanity, because once my kids got up, it was over. I scheduled regular appointments with a trainer to keep me accountable and alleviate the mental energy I'd otherwise spend on working out on my own. I hired a personal assistant to help me manage my emails and schedule and to run small errands. I hired a children's sleep therapist—which I totally recommend—to help us achieve a more structured routine. And I joined Entrepreneurs' Organization, which gave me personal and professional support as a business owner. On top of the professionals I hired, I also found help with meal prepping. My own company's products were my saving grace, and I became my own best customer, which was incredibly validating.

By delegating tasks and making time to support my spiritual and mental health, I was able to accomplish more. Still, it was several months before I felt as if I could breathe again, and in time, I found my grounding and reincorporated my self-serving habits to manage and support my healthy lifestyle. In hindsight, I'd taken on too much too fast, and as any momma knows, Momma just needs time to be Momma, to take care of herself. And at night, I could be present with my family, which is still one of my top priorities.

Getting your priorities in order is how you will find the time. If you want your life to be awesome, take full ownership of everything required to make room to support new habits. I knew that by shifting my schedule, I could find time to learn, grow, and adapt. It wasn't following a diet, it was changing my routine such that I could maintain the mental capacity to figure out how to eat healthy. Diets are short-lived; lifestyle changes are what make changing the way you eat and live sustainable. Step back and look at the bigger picture. Take ownership of everything and manage it to its fullest potential.

If you don't have time now, you are going to have to make time, or find peace and be patient in your current season of life. Life isn't perfect, and making a lifestyle change doesn't happen overnight. When we learn to show ourselves grace—which is a process in itself—we accept our harder days as, well, harder days, not as failures. We stay positive and make the next day count and keep going. Showing grace is a commitment to consistency, not perfection. There will be times that life isn't what you think it should be, but that's life, so own that. Each brick you lay for the castle you are building is a step in the right direction. My castle is dynamic—full of people, products, children, spirituality, financials, fun, wellness, and more. Some days, I make good progress and build a new room, whereas other days, the walls are falling down. It's a process, and the castle requires upkeep.

To help you discover where you can find/make time in your busy schedule, consider the following questions and recommendations:

- Can you wake up earlier or stay up later? Are you an early bird or night owl? Work to your strengths. Schedule your time better so you can work and grow when it is most effective. Make sure to get at least seven or eight hours of sleep, if possible.
- Can you get more strict with your schedule and set boundaries? Saying no to less important things is saying yes to your priorities.

- Can you sacrifice your leisure/TV/friends/play time? Maybe it's just for a season of life. Managing your out-of-balance life is a way of leveling up. All truly successful people have sacrificed to get ahead.

- Can you hire a professional to free up headspace? If you think that it costs too much, you may be trapped by short-term thinking. It's not what it costs—it's what you can make or do with that time or help.

- Can you stop doing something that doesn't serve your goals? This can be hard, as you have to look at yourself in the mirror and ask the hard questions, then be humble enough to do the right thing. Don't let your ego get in the way.

- Can you find mental, emotional, and spiritual support for the new life you are trying to live? If you skip this part, sustaining results will be much harder.

The reality is that life is chaotic. It throws us curveballs. Learning to manage life while keeping your mind right is a part of the training. "This too shall pass"—so do your best to keep moving forward.

OWNING AND PROCESSING THE FAILURES

"[Failure] doesn't define you, it's just a problem to be faced, dealt with, and learned from."
— *Carol Dweck, PhD*

How we view failure is a common conversation topic among those pursuing a healthy lifestyle. The word *failure* may sound negative, but with the never-ending program that is a healthy lifestyle, you can't truly fail unless you completely stop nurturing your well-being. And the word *failure* resonates with me because it helps to destigmatize what is a normal part of personal growth, and putting my failures into perspective helps me to move past them more efficiently.

Furthermore, eating one less-healthy meal does not constitute a failure; maybe you were unprepared and just needed to eat, or maybe you opted in to your 20 percent. You can strive to make better decisions going forward, mindful of the 80–20 balance. And don't you want to be present when you opt in to your 20 percent? Aren't desserts meant to be enjoyed, not suffered? This also revisits the on/off trap, wherein a person can let one small failure define their whole day or week as "off," promising themselves they'll start fresh in "on" mode tomorrow or next week. When I hear that, I think to myself, *Start what?! You don't have to be perfect, so just strive to do a little better all the time.*

No one can promise you a perfect outcome. What I can tell you is that when you take small, positive steps at your own pace over time, they usually add up to a comeback or a win. At the end of the day, most people who win are the ones that take ownership, work hard, and show up—consistently. The sooner you realize that, the sooner you'll start making progress, regardless of any mini failures along the way.

When it comes to nutrition, many people struggle with getting it right. Heck, that's why I started my business and why I wrote this book. I had heard enough people talking about how fad diets with restrictive rules overpromise results and perpetuate unrealistic stereotypes, making failure both hit harder and be more likely to happen. (Remember that if you have a health condition or an allergy, changing your diet to accommodate those restrictions is a vital part of supporting your continued health.) It's not that the fad diets don't work; it's that they don't work long-term.

Because fad diets are short-lived, people fail at them more often than they succeed. In this context, the word *failure* is relative, because people can just decide to be done with a diet and go back to how things used to be, until they decide to start yet another diet. In the long term, it is much more sustainable to focus on better overall eating and on customizing your plan to your lifestyle, because there is no end, no finish date, to this new way of life. The pursuit of healthy living goes on every day, until you die. (Well, that's the goal, right?)

I understand the drive to lose that extra five pounds or tighten up before going on vacation, or for a challenge at the gym, but why would you want to look and feel better only while on vacation or for a challenge? Wouldn't you prefer to be happy with your body all the time? If all you're looking for is a small boost in motivation, more power to you, but don't let the narratives that come with meeting a short-term goal affect you mentally. Know what the heck you are doing—and *why*. After years of yo-yoing, I finally ditched the short-term approach and decided I was going to follow the 80–20 rule indefinitely, and I haven't looked back. I still fail all the time, but it's mostly small stuff, and I can always do better tomorrow.

Processing failure is the humble recognition of where work and focus are needed. After you've sobbed and sulked, it's time to get to work! Process your failure, learn from it, and use those lessons as you continue striving forward. Be humble and accept where you went wrong, both physically and mentally. If you're feeling angry or disappointed with yourself, harness that energy and dial it in to the positive steps you need to take to get back on track. Failures don't define you—they shape you. They show you where you need to focus and reevaluate. They are experiences to be learned from. Failing may knock you off track, but it's about how fast you get back up and keep going. Don't sulk. Don't be lazy. Don't be a victim. Fully owning your failures serves you, and it is in your best interest to not let pride get in the way of processing them. When you own and process your failures, that's when you grow.

TRUSTING THE PROCESS

Trusting the process frees us of stress and guilt and allows us to experience hope, peace, and happiness.

Trusting the process is having faith in the science and making peace with the time it is going to take to achieve your goals. It really is the last step in making sustainable long-term changes in your lifestyle.

I get it—it's hard to trust, to have faith, in something you've yet to experience. Even after you finish this book, it will probably take you a while to process the information and begin to determine how to best go about making the changes you desire. Even after reading my story, some of you may still be in denial about this process. And that's OK—I was, too, years ago.

You'll recall that I let my false narratives run my life for quite some time. It was only after I took ownership of my mindset and my decisions that I was able to see a path forward. I shifted my schedule to support change. I worked hard to learn about nutrition and fitness. I made small changes at my own pace to develop healthier habits, eventually getting to the point where managing an 80–20 balance was almost reflexive. Each time I ate, each time I worked out, each time I made time to learn—those were all small steps in the right direction. And by putting in the work to develop healthy, supportive habits, I've been better able to weather the obstacles that life has thrown at me and my business, such as the COVID-19 pandemic. None of that would have been possible had I not trusted the process. Because of that, I was able to achieve my goals of being at peace with food choices, losing weight with proper nutrition, and living a healthy life—plus, I get to eat more french fries!

This "trusting the process" doesn't happen quickly, either. These steps are not boxes you get to check off. I want to be very transparent, so it bears repeating—these steps happen over time as you make one good decision followed by another, and another, and so on. That's how you create change. Change is you—your whole being—not just your waistline. Positive changes breed confidence for the mindset and allow you to trust the process more and more. It takes consistent work to create impact. And that, my friend, takes time. So chill out with the deadlines and be patient.

In the end, this is no different than putting in the extra hours to advance in your career, knowing that the work and time will lead to a bright and fulfilling future. When you're in the thick of it, it can be hard to tell if you're even getting any traction, and you may even feel like quitting. But the amount of effort you put forth will determine the results. If you can align your narratives and get educated, you will be on the right track to achieve success.

I remember when I was in the thick of a huge growth spurt with fit-flavors. We were entering our seventh year, and I had been struggling for the past three—I wanted to throw in the towel. Plagued by negative emotions and physical stress, I often thought about quitting. But I didn't, instead continuing to take action to move forward. Looking back on that long struggle, I am very proud of the positive strides we made as a company in those three years. I didn't see it then, but the amazing work we did set us up nicely for where we are today. That is a huge example of trusting the process when the world feels against you.

Getting educated takes time—we all know that. Learning is part of growing, and that includes gaining the confidence and courage to do what is right and trust it will work. I see customers I've known for years that are now living healthier lives, yet they're still working hard to be more consistent in their never-ending pursuit to do a little better each day. It's about consistency—I can't say that enough!

WHAT'S NEXT

You might feel good after reading this book because you feel like you have a better understanding of what you need to do. If so, great! I think part of the reason we feel good after finishing a book is because it's as if we experienced the book with the author. You might even feel motivated now, but that will dissipate, and your habits and disciplines will need to be efficient so you can create your own motivation.

Even though you're in the same relative place you were when you started reading, I bet you learned something, so kudos—one brick closer to building your castle! If you aren't where you want to be, remember that the healthier person you are becoming is your goal. As your mindset and character change, your happiness and fulfillment will follow. But what about now? Well, you've read my story. Now it's time for you to write your story. It will be very different from mine.

If you didn't already take time to do the visual or the narrative exercises, do those first. Then find some awesome resources to help you level up your nutrition knowledge. I will shamelessly plug fit-flavors, as we have an online course called fitU—created by our licensed and registered dietitian—which is designed to reeducate you on nutrition and shift your approach to making lifestyle changes. The course is a long-term alternative to every fad diet. There are a ton of other great resources out there for personal development; all you need to do is start reading or listening to them regularly. And give yourself at least a year to start seeing any sustainable results.

As for practicing grace, get yourself a journal or planner. You need to have some kind of outlet to help manage your spiritual and emotional well-being through this change. Again, making time to do this for yourself is a step in a process. Like I said, for me, time with God is huge, and a lot of my development and truth has come from the Bible. I've read a ton of personal-development books, and I still read them. One of my favorites is *Mindset : The New Psychology of Success* by Carol Dweck. That book helped me overcome my fear of not being smart enough, which ultimately led to my being a better leader and continuing to learn.

Now get to work on you!